REMAIN SANE: LIGHT AND SHADOW

The Sane Bloodline Saga — Book I

Alonzo Bazemore Sr.

Copyright Page

ISBN: 979-8-9977195-1-7

Publisher: BazeWorks Wellness & Media

Printed in the United States of America

Contents

Acknowledgements

This book is dedicated to people whose love, strength, and memory that shaped every page.

To my grandmother, Clara Edwards, to my sister, Ramona Koon, and to my father, James Bazemore Sr., who are now resting in heaven. Your lives, your lessons, and your spirits walk with me every day. I authored this story with you in my heart, and I carry you with me in every step I take.

To my wife, Nettie, who has stood by my side for seventeen years. Your loyalty, your patience, and your love have been my anchor. You believed in me long before I believed in myself, and this book exists because you never let me quit.

To my children, Alonzo Jr., Dylan, and Logan, who give me strength every single day. You inspire me to be better today than I was yesterday, and to look forward to tomorrow with purpose. Your love is my fuel. Your smiles are my hope. Your future is my motivation.

This book has been twenty years in the making. It has been my passion project, my escape, my therapy, and my mission. It was inspired by the people I am passionate about who shaped me, supported me, and taught me what it means to fight, to endure, and to love.

To everyone named here: This story is yours as much as mine.

PROLOGUE — THE VOICE IN THE CLASSROOM

Roman Sane was six years old when he first heard the voice.

It did not come from the teacher, or the hallway, or the world outside the classroom windows where Baltimore buses groaned past like tired beasts. It came from somewhere deeper, somewhere older, somewhere that felt like it had been waiting for him long before he was born.

What kind of man will you become, Roman?

What will you do when the world shows you its teeth?

The voice was calm. Too calm.

It spoke like someone who already knew the answers.

Roman blinked, his small hands frozen above the worksheet on his desk. The classroom around him blurred, the chatter of children fading into a low hum. For a moment, he wasn't in school at all. He was suspended in a strange, heavy silence one that felt like the air before a storm.

Then the laughter cut through it.

A spitball smacked the back of his neck. Another hit his cheek. Ryan and Terrell—two boys who had decided Roman was their entertainment for the week snickered behind their hands, straws still wet with spit.

Roman didn't move at first. He just stared ahead, jaw tightening, breath slowing. Something inside him shifted something he didn't have a name for yet.

You don't have to take that, the voice murmured.

You were not made to bow.

Roman stood so fast, his chair screeched across the floor.

"You wanna fight me?" he shouted, his voice cracking with rage. "Then let's go, bitch!"

The classroom froze.

The teacher gasped.

And Roman felt… awake.

Minutes later, he sat in the principal's office, legs dangling off the chair, face blank. The adults asked him questions about his home life, his feelings, his behavior. Roman answered each one with the same practiced calm he had learned far too early.

He knew the rules.

He knew what they wanted to hear.

He knew no one was coming to save him.

Outside, the city waited for him and his sister Langley—eight years old, sharp as broken glass, already learning how to survive in ways Roman didn't yet understand. Baltimore was a place of contradictions: beauty and rot, hope and violence, saints and monsters living on the same block.

Roman didn't know which one he was yet.

But the voice did.

As he and Langley walked home, Ryan and Terrell appeared again, hurling insults. Roman tried to ignore them, he really did until Ryan shoved him.

The world went red.

Roman tackled him, fists flying, each punch landing with a clarity that terrified him and thrilled him at the same time. Terrell tried to pull him off, and Roman's hand moved on instinct, grabbing the pencil in his pocket and driving it into Terrell's leg.

Langley dragged him away, breathless, furious, protective.

Roman didn't speak.

He couldn't.

Because for the first time in his young life, he understood something:

He was not like other children.

He was something else.

Something dangerous.

Good, the voice whispered.

Now you're beginning to see.

That night, Roman sat alone in his room, staring at his hands. He felt the weight of what he had done, but he also felt something darker, something that made his heart beat faster.

He felt powerful.

And somewhere deep inside him, the voice smiled.

CHAPTER 1 — THE BEST-LAID PLANS

Morning sunlight crept through the blinds of Roman Sane's bedroom, cutting thin golden lines across the sheets tangled around him and Corinne. The world outside was quiet, but inside Roman's mind, the same old hum lingered…the faint echo of a voice he had spent decades trying to ignore.

You can't outrun what you are.

He exhaled slowly, grounding himself in the warmth of Corinne's body pressed against him. Her breath rose and fell against his chest, steady and soft, a rhythm that had saved him more times than she knew. She shifted, her lips brushing his skin, and for a moment the voice faded.

Corinne Baxter was the kind of woman who made the world feel survivable. Strong, brilliant, disciplined yet gentle in ways Roman had never believed he deserved. She kissed him again, deeper this time, and the morning dissolved into heat, breath, and the kind of intimacy that made Roman forget the darkness he carried.

When they finally collapsed beside each other, Corinne laughed softly.

"Aren't you supposed to be getting ready for your flight?"

Roman smirked. "Trying to kick me out already?"

She nudged him with her shoulder. "No. But you know how you get when you're late. And I'm not listening to you complain about traffic again."

He chuckled, rolling out of bed. "I'm hitting the gym today. Tournament's coming up."

Corinne sat up, tying her hair back. "You want me to drop you off?"

"Nah. Dom's got me."

She kissed him once more before heading out the door, her heels clicking against the hardwood floor. Roman watched her leave, a quiet pride swelling in his chest. Corinne had fought her way out of poverty, war, and loss to become an Assistant District Attorney. She was a survivor like him, but her strength was clean, bright, untainted.

Roman's was not.

THE STATION

The roll call room at Kings Horn Police District buzzed with tension the moment Roman stepped inside. Officers straightened in their seats, some out of respect, others out of resentment. Roman felt it all—the admiration, the skepticism, the quiet hostility.

He had been promoted fast. Too fast, according to some.

But Roman didn't care. He had earned every stripe, every scar, every sleepless night.

He stood at the podium, scanning the room.

They don't trust you, the voice whispered.

Good. Trust is a weakness.

Roman ignored it.

"Good morning," he began, his tone steady. "I'm Major Sane. Before you head out, I want to leave you with this: change starts here. With you. With the choices you make when no one is watching."

Some officers nodded. Others stared blankly. A few glared.

Roman continued anyway. "I don't want clones. I want leaders. I want the best of what each of you brings to this department. Be smart. Be intentional. And above all else be safe."

He stepped back, nodding to the sergeant. "It's all yours."

As he walked to his office, the voice returned low, amused.

They fear you. They should.

Roman shut the door behind him and sat at his desk, staring at the framed photo of Corinne and their four children. Two boys. Two girls. A life he had clawed his way toward. A life he still wasn't sure he deserved.

"How did I get here?" he whispered.

You didn't, the voice murmured. You stole it.

Roman stiffened.

A knock broke the silence. Captain James Bazemore stepped inside, Roman's oldest friend, the only person who knew even a fraction of the truth.

"You good?" James asked. "You look pale."

Roman forced a breath. "Just tired."

James didn't buy it, but he let it go. "We've got a situation. Reggie Hepper turned himself in. Says he wants to talk to you."

Roman froze.

Reggie Hepper was a ghost, a kingpin who had slipped through the justice system for years. He didn't turn himself in. He didn't surrender. He didn't ask for anyone.

Especially not Roman.

Roman stood. "Let's go."

Hepper sat alone, hands folded neatly, a smile carved across his face like a wound.

"Major Sane," he drawled. "Been a long time."

Roman didn't sit. "Why are you here?"

"Three reasons," Hepper said. "One…I wanted to see you. Two…how's Langley? And three…hire more officers. Your crew looks thin."

Roman's jaw tightened. "You're being detained for questioning."

Hepper laughed. "You motherfucker! You weren't always blue, Roman. Don't forget I know the real you."

Roman left the room without another word.

James caught up with him. "What was that about?"

"I don't know," Roman muttered. "But it's not good."

His phone buzzed. A voicemail.

His mother's voice—broken, trembling.

"Roman… baby… it's your mom. I have tragic news… your sister Langley is dead…"

The world tilted.

The voice inside him whispered:

It begins.

Roman didn't remember leaving the station. One moment he was staring at Hepper's twisted grin, the next he was behind the wheel of his car, the city blurring past him in streaks of gray and red. His mother's voicemail replayed in his mind, each word cutting deeper than the last.

Your sister Langley is dead…

Dead.

The word didn't fit her. Langley wasn't someone who died. She was someone who survived, someone who bent the world to her will, someone who carved her name into the streets of East Baltimore with equal parts brilliance and brutality.

If Langley was dead, then something unnatural would have happened.

And Roman felt it deep in the place where the voice lived.

You knew this day would come, it whispered.

You just didn't want to believe it.

Roman gripped the steering wheel until his knuckles whitened. "Shut up," he muttered.

But the voice only chuckled.

ROMAN'S MOTHER'S HOUSE

The moment Roman stepped inside, the air hit him like a physical force thick with grief, fear, and the metallic scent of blood. His mother was on the kitchen floor, sobbing in her hands. Kaye and Cage stood near the back door, their clothes stained, their eyes hollow.

Roman's pulse spiked. "What the hell happened?

Kaye swallowed hard. "They pulled up on us out of nowhere. Masks. Rifles. They… they emptied the whole clip into her, Rome. We couldn't—"

Cage cut in, voice flat, dead. "She's gone. And they took her body."

Roman's vision tunneled.

Not from shock, he wasn't shocked.

From rage.

A cold, ancient rage that didn't feel entirely human.

He lunged at Cage, grabbing him by the throat and lifting him off the ground with a strength that startled even him.

"WHO THE HELL IS THEY?" Roman roared.

Cage's eyes darkened, his own violence rising to meet Roman's. He redirected Roman's grip and swung, but Roman slipped the punch effortlessly, throwing Cage across the kitchen like he weighed nothing.

Kaye stepped between them. "Enough! Your mother is breaking down and your sister is missing. This is not the time!"

Roman opened his mouth to respond…

and the world exploded.

A thunderous blast shook the house, shattering windows and throwing everyone to the floor. Roman's ears rang, his vision flickered, and for a moment he couldn't tell if he was alive or dead.

Then the screaming started.

Roman staggered to his feet, drawing his weapon on instinct. He moved toward the front door, each step heavy, each breath sharp.

Outside, the world had changed.

THE BEGINNING OF THE END

The street was in chaos with buildings burning, cars overturned, people running in every direction. Smoke curled into the sky like black serpents. The air tasted like ash and fear.

And then Roman saw them.

Figures emerging through the smoke twisted, staggering, wrong. Their movements were jerky, their bodies contorted, their skin pale and cracked like old stone. Their eyes were empty, but their mouths hung open in silent hunger.

Not human.

Not alive.

Not possible.

Cage stepped beside him, trembling. "What… what the hell are those things?"

Roman didn't answer.

Because the voice inside him did.

They are the beginning, Roman.

And you were born for the end.

Roman's jaw clenched. "Get my mother to the truck. Now."

Kaye and Cage obeyed, dragging her toward the vehicle as Roman opened the trunk and grabbed his tactical vest and AR-15. He loaded the weapon with practiced precision, his mind eerily calm.

The creatures shrieked an inhuman, piercing sound that made Roman's bones vibrate. They charged.

Roman fired.

Rounds tore through the first wave but more came. Dozens. Maybe hundreds. The street became a battlefield, and Roman moved through it like he had been training for this moment his entire life.

One creature lunged at him, jaws snapping. Roman drew his sidearm and fired point-blank, dropping it instantly.

He didn't feel fear.

He didn't panic.

He felt… clarity.

Good, the voice whispered.

Now you're waking up.

Roman climbed into the truck, slamming the door behind him. "Drive!"

As they sped toward the station, the city burned behind them.

And Roman knew deep in the marrow of his bones that this was only the beginning.

CHAPTER 2 — THE STATION UNDER SIEGE

The truck tore down the ruined street, tires skidding over broken glass and debris. Roman kept his eyes on the road, but his mind was split half focused on survival, half spiraling into a storm of questions he wasn't ready to face.

His mother sat in the back seat, trembling, her hands pressed to her mouth. Kaye held her steady, whispering reassurances he didn't believe. Cage sat rigid in the passenger seat, staring out the window at the burning city with a look Roman had seen only a few times before—when Cage was seconds away from doing something reckless.

Roman's grip tightened on the wheel.

"Don't," he said quietly.

Cage didn't look at him. "Don't what?"

"Don't go looking for a fight you can't win."

Cage scoffed. "You think I'm scared of those things?"

Roman didn't answer.

Because fear wasn't the problem.

Cage wasn't afraid of dying.

He was afraid of being powerless.

And Roman understood that better than anyone.

THE STATION UNDER SIEGE

As they approached the Kings Horn Police District, Roman's stomach dropped. Smoke billowed from the building. Patrol cars were overturned. The front windows were shattered. Officers were firing from behind barricades, their shouts drowned out by the shrieks of the creatures swarming the parking lot.

James Bazemore stood at the entrance, directing officers with the calm intensity of a man who had seen war and refused to break.

Roman slammed the truck to a stop. "Get my mother inside. Now!"

Kaye and Cage helped her out, shielding her as they ran toward the station. Roman grabbed his rifle and stepped out, firing controlled bursts at the creatures closing in.

James spotted him. "Roman! What the hell is happening?"

Roman didn't know how to answer. He didn't know what these things were, where they came from, or why the world had turned into a nightmare in a matter of minutes.

But the voice inside him did.

This is the reckoning, Roman.

The world is shedding its skin.

And you… you were made for what comes next.

Roman ignored it, focusing on the fight. He and James moved in sync, covering each other as they pushed toward the entrance. Officers dragged wounded colleagues inside. The creatures clawed at the barricades, their bodies jerking unnaturally, their movements too fast, too erratic.

Roman fired until his magazine clicked empty.

Then he switched to his sidearm.

Then to his knife.

He didn't think.

He didn't hesitate.

He didn't fear it.

He moved like a man possessed.

And maybe he was.

INSIDE THE STATION

The doors slammed behind them, officers pushing desks and filing cabinets against the entrance. The station was dimly lit, emergency lights flickering overhead. Radios crackled with static. Someone was crying. Someone else was praying.

James grabbed Roman's arm. "Talk to me. What did you see out there?"

Roman wiped blood he wasn't sure who's from his cheek. "Not human."

James stared at him. "You're telling me we're dealing with what? Zombies?"

Roman didn't answer.

Because the word felt wrong.

Too simple.

Too childish.

These things weren't mindless.

They weren't slow.

They weren't dead.

They were something else.

Something older.

Something hungry.

Before Roman could speak, the lights flickered again. The building shook. A deep, guttural roar echoed from outside louder than the shrieks, louder than the gunfire, loud enough to make the walls vibrate.

Officers froze.

James whispered, "What the hell was that?"

Roman felt the voice inside him stir, almost… pleased.

The first king awakened; it murmured.

And soon, Roman, you will meet him.

Roman's breath caught in his throat.

Because for the first time since he was six years old…

He wasn't sure the voice was lying.

THE CALL THAT CHANGED EVERYTHING

Before Roman could process the roar, his phone buzzed again.

Another voicemail.

He hesitated.

James noticed. "Who is it?"

Roman swallowed. "My mother called earlier. About Langley."

James's expression softened. "I'm sorry, man. I know you two—"

"She's not dead," Roman said quietly.

James blinked. "Roman… you heard your mother."

Roman shook his head. "No. Something's wrong. Langley doesn't go out like that. Not without a message. Not without a war."

James hesitated. "You think she's alive?"

Roman didn't answer.

Because the voice inside him whispered:

She is not dead, Roman.

She has simply crossed into the dark before you.

And you will follow.

Roman closed his eyes.

And for the first time in his life…

He wasn't sure if the voice was warning him.

Or calling him home.

CHAPTER 3 — THE FIRST BREACH

The station trembled again, dust drifting from the ceiling like falling ash. Officers exchanged fearful glances, their nerves stretched thin. The roar outside had changed something in the room, shifted the air, thickened it, made it harder to breathe.

Roman felt it in his bones.

Not fear.

Recognition.

James placed a hand on his shoulder. "Roman… what aren't you telling me?"

Roman didn't answer. He couldn't. Because the truth wasn't something he could explain not without sounding insane, not without opening doors he had spent his entire life trying to keep sealed.

But the voice inside him whispered anyway.

You've always known, Roman. You've always felt the world beneath the world. The rot under the skin. The truth behind the lie.

Roman clenched his jaw. "We need to secure the building. Get everyone to the armory. Lock down the perimeter."

James nodded, slipping into command mode. "You heard him! Move!"

Officers scrambled, forming defensive positions. The station's emergency lights flickered again, casting the room in a pulsing red glow that made every shadow look alive.

Roman moved through the chaos with a strange calm. His mind was sharp, focused, almost… elevated. The fear around him didn't touch him. The panic didn't reach him.

If anything, the danger made him feel more like himself.

THE FIRST BREACH

A deafening crash shook the front entrance. The barricaded doors buckled inward, metal groaning under the force of something slamming against them from the outside.

Officers raised their weapons.

James shouted, "Hold the line!"

Another slam.

Then another.

Then a long, dragging scrape like claws raking across steel.

Roman stepped forward, rifle raised.

The voice inside him purred.

Let them come.

The doors exploded inward.

Creatures poured through the opening twisted silhouettes with jerking limbs and hollow eyes. Their movements were too fast, too violent, too wrong. Officers opened fire, bullets tearing through flesh that barely seemed to notice the damage.

Roman fired with precision, dropping targets one by one. But for every creature that fell, two more took its place.

James shouted over the gunfire, "Fall back! Fall back to the armory!"

Roman didn't move.

He stood on his ground, firing until his rifle clicked empty. Then he drew his sidearm. Then his knife. His movements were fluid, instinctive, and almost inhumanly efficient.

James grabbed his arm. "Roman! Move!"

Roman blinked, snapping out of the trance. He followed James down the hallway as officers slammed the armory door shut behind them, locking it with shaking hands.

Inside, the room was dim, lit only by a few flickering bulbs. Officers reloaded, tended to wounds, whispered prayers.

Roman stood apart, breathing hard, staring at the blood on his hands.

Not all of it was his.

Not all of it was theirs.

Some of them felt older.

THE REVELATION

James approached him quietly. "Roman… what's happening to you?"

Roman didn't look at him. "I don't know."

But he did know.

He just didn't want to say it.

James lowered his voice. "You fought like you knew what they were. Like you've seen this before.

Roman's eyes darkened. "I haven't."

The voice inside him laughed softly.

Liar.

Roman pressed a hand to his forehead, trying to silence it. But the voice only grew clearer.

You were born for this, Roman. Born from violence. Forged in chaos. You are not prey. You are not victim. You are the blade that cuts the dark.

Roman's breath hitched.

James stepped closer. "Talk to me, man. I'm right here."

Roman finally met his eyes.

"There's something wrong with me."

James didn't flinch. "There always has been. But you're still my brother."

Roman almost smiled. Almost.

Then the station shook again harder than before.

A roar echoed through the halls, deeper and more powerful than the last. Officers froze. Weapons trembled in their hands.

Roman felt the sound vibrate through his chest, through his bones, through the part of him he had spent his entire life trying to bury.

The voice inside him whispered:

He is coming.

Roman's heart pounded.

"Who?" he whispered under his breath.

The voice answered:

The one who killed your sister.

Roman's blood ran cold.

And for the first time since the world began to fall apart…

He felt fear.

CHAPTER 4 — THE DARKNESS PRESSES IN

The armory door rattled again, harder this time, as if something massive pressed its weight against the other side. Officers backed away instinctively, their fear thick enough to taste. The emergency lights flickered overhead, bathing the room in a pulsing red glow that made every face look hollow and bloodless.

Roman stood perfectly still.

Not because he wasn't afraid.

But because the fear felt… familiar.

James watched him carefully. "Roman… talk to me. What's going on inside your head?"

Roman didn't answer.

Because the truth was worse than anything he could say out loud.

Inside his mind, the voice was no longer whispering.

It was pacing.

You feel it, don't you? The shift. The thinning of the veil. The world is cracking open, Roman, and everything buried beneath it is crawling to the surface.

Roman pressed his palms against the metal table, grounding himself. His breath came slow, controlled but his pulse hammered like a war drum.

James stepped closer. "You're shaking."

Roman hadn't realized he was.

He clenched his fists until his knuckles whitened. "I'm fine."

The voice laughed at a low, ancient sound that curled around his spine like smoke.

You are not fine. You are awakening.

Roman's vision blurred for a moment. The room dimmed. The officers' voices faded. And in the corner of the armory, where the shadows pooled thickest, he saw movement.

A silhouette.

Tall.

Wrong.

Watching him.

Roman blinked and it vanished.

He swallowed hard. "James… something's coming."

James nodded. "Yeah. I heard the roar."

"No," Roman said quietly. "Not outside. Here. For me."

James stared at him, confused. "Why you?"

Roman didn't know how to answer.

Because the truth was something he had never admitted not even to himself.

The creatures outside didn't feel foreign.

They didn't feel random.

They didn't feel like they were in an accident.

They felt like a message.

A message meant for him.

THE DARKNESS PRESSES IN

The armory lights flickered again, plunging the room into darkness for a full second. When they came back on, several officers gasped.

Because the shadows on the far wall had changed.

They were longer.

Sharper.

Twisted into shapes that didn't match the bodies casting them.

James whispered, "Roman… do you see that?"

Roman didn't answer.

Because the shadows were moving.

Slowly.

Deliberately.

Like they were breathing.

The voice inside him purred.

They recognize you. Even before you recognize yourself.

Roman's heart pounded. "Stop."

Why? You've always known you were different. Stronger. Faster. Angrier. You thought it was trauma. You thought it was survival. But it was destiny.

Roman's breath hitched.

James grabbed his arm. "Roman. Look at me."

Roman forced himself to meet his friend's eyes.

"You're not alone," James said. "Whatever this is, we'll face it together."

Roman wanted to believe him.

But the voice whispered:

He cannot follow you where you are going.

THE SECOND BREACH

A thunderous impact shook the station, knocking weapons off racks and sending officers stumbling. The roar that followed was deeper than before — so deep Roman felt it in his teeth.

The armory door bent inward, metal warping like soft clay.

Officers screamed.

Guns were raised.

Someone began praying.

James stepped in front of Roman, with his weapon drawn. "Whatever's out there… it's not getting to you."

Roman almost laughed.

Not because it was funny.

But because it was pointless.

The thing outside wasn't trying to get in.

It was trying to get him.

The voice inside him confirmed it.

He smells you, Roman. He remembers your blood. He remembers your sister's. And he is coming to finish what he started.

Roman's stomach twisted. "Langley…"

James's eyes widened. "You think the thing that killed her is out there?"

Roman didn't answer.

Because the truth was worse:

He didn't think it.

He knew it.

The armory door buckled again this time leaving a deep dent in the steel.

Officers backed away, panic rising.

James whispered, "Roman… what do we do?"

Roman stepped forward.

Toward the door.

Toward the roar.

Toward the darkness calling his name.

"We open it," he said quietly.

James grabbed him. "Are you insane?!"

Roman's eyes were cold.

Focused.

Unshaken.

"No," he said. "I'm done running."

The voice inside him smiled.

Good. Let the darkness in.

CHAPTER 5 — BLOOD OF THE FIRST

The armory door groaned again, but this time the sound was different less like metal under pressure and more like something breathing against it. A slow, rhythmic exhale that made the hair on every officer's neck stand on end.

James whispered, "Roman… that's not an animal."

Roman didn't respond.

Because he already knew.

The voice inside him the one that had haunted him since childhood had gone silent.

Not gone.

Not absent.

Silent.

Like it was listening.

The temperature in the room dropped. Officers' breaths fogged in the air. The emergency lights flickered, then dimmed to a low, pulsing red that made the shadows stretch unnaturally long across the walls.

And then the shadows began to move.

Not fast.

Not violently.

Slowly.

Deliberately.

Like they were waking up.

One shadow detached itself from the wall, stretching upward until it formed the outline of a tall, distorted figure. Its limbs were too long. Its head tilted to an unnatural angle. And though it had no eyes, Roman felt it staring directly at him.

James stepped back, voice trembling. "Roman… what the hell is that?"

Roman's throat tightened.

Because he had seen this shape before.

In dreams.

In nightmares.

In the corner of his childhood bedroom when he was too afraid to sleep.

The voice inside him finally spoke but it wasn't a whisper anymore.

It was reverent.

He has found you.

Roman's pulse spiked. "Who?"

The shadow figure twitched, its form rippling like smoke caught in the wind only it could feel. The armory door behind it buckled inward again, but this time the impact wasn't random.

It was rhythmic.

Intentional.

Like knocking.

James raised his weapon. "Roman, we need to fall back. Now."

Roman didn't move.

Because the shadow stepped closer.

And when it did, every officer in the room felt something press against their minds — a cold, invasive pressure that made several of them drop to their knees, clutching their heads.

James gasped. "Roman… it's inside my—"

Roman grabbed him, steadying him. "Don't let it in."

But the truth was brutal:

It wasn't trying to get into James.

It was trying to get into Roman.

The shadow's form rippled again, and a low, distorted voice filled the room not through sound, but through thought.

"Blood of the First.

Child of the Rift.

We have waited."

Roman staggered back, breath catching in his throat. "No… no, that's not me."

The shadow tilted its head.

"You were marked at birth.

You were chosen.

You were promised."

James stared at Roman, horrified. "Promised? Roman, what is it talking about?"

Roman shook his head violently. "I don't know. I don't…"

The voice inside him cut him off.

You do know. You've always known. You just didn't want to believe it.

The armory door dented inward again — this time with a force that sent cracks spiderwebbing across the steel.

Officers screamed.

Weapons shook.

The air vibrated.

The shadow figure extended an elongated arm toward Roman.

"Come, Heir of Sane.

Your blood calls the King."

Roman's heart stopped.

Because the name "Sane" wasn't just his last name.

It was a lineage.

A legacy.

A curse.

James grabbed Roman's arm. "We're leaving. Now."

But Roman couldn't move.

Because the shadow's final words weren't spoken to the room.

They were spoken directly into Roman's mind.

"Your sister crossed first.

Now you must follow."

Roman's breath shattered.

"Langley…"

The shadow nodded slowly.

"She is not dead.

She is becoming."

The armory door exploded inward.

And the King stepped through.

CHAPTER 6 — THE KING STEPS THROUGH

The King stepped through the shattered doorway, and the air itself recoiled.

He was enormous not in size, but in presence. His silhouette flickered like a dying flame, shifting between forms: a towering humanoid shape, a horned beast, a mass of writhing shadows. His body was not fresh. It was suggestion. A shape the mind struggled to hold.

Officers screamed.

Some fired.

Some dropped their weapons and fell to their knees.

But Roman…

Roman couldn't move.

Because the King wasn't looking at the officers.

He wasn't looking at James.

He wasn't looking at the room.

He was looking at him.

The voice inside Roman… the one that had whispered to him his entire life, didn't speak.

It bowed.

Roman felt it.

A bending.

A yielding.

A submission.

The King's voice filled the room, not through sound, but through the marrow of every bone.

"At last."

James staggered backward, clutching his head. "Roman… what is he saying? Roman, what the hell is he saying?!"

Roman didn't answer.

Because the King's words weren't meant for James.

They were meant for him alone.

"Blood of the First.

Child of the Rift.

Bearer of the Mark."

Roman's breath caught. "No… no, that's not me."

The King stepped closer, and the shadows bent toward him like worshippers.

"It is you.

It has always been you."

Roman's vision blurred. Memories he didn't recognize flashed behind his eyes a battlefield of fire and ash, a throne of bone, a crown of black iron. A woman screaming his name. A blade dripping with something darker than blood.

James grabbed Roman's arm. "Roman! Snap out of it!"

Roman jerked away, eyes wide. "Don't touch me."

James froze.

Because Roman's voice didn't sound like his own.

It sounded layered two voices speaking at once.

His… and something older.

The King tilted his head, studying Roman with a grotesque fascination.

"You hear us.

You feel us.

You carry us."

Roman shook his head violently. "Get out of my mind."

The King's form rippled, and the shadows behind him writhed like serpents.

"We are not in your mind.

We are of your mind."

Roman's stomach twisted.

Because deep down, he knew it was true.

The voice he had heard since childhood, the one he thought was trauma, imagination, madness wasn't a hallucination.

It was a tether.

A connection.

A birthright.

James stepped between them, raised weapons. "I don't know what you are, but you're not taking him."

The King didn't even look at him.

"He is already taken."

Roman felt something inside him shift a pull, gravity, a dark warmth spreading through his chest like ink in water. His heartbeat slowed. His vision sharpened. The room dimmed around the edges, as if the world itself were stepping back to make space for something else.

James saw the change. "Roman… your eyes."

Roman blinked.

His irises had darkened not black, but something deeper, something bottomless. Like looking into a well with no end.

The King extended a hand.

Not to strike.

Not to kill.

To welcome.

"Come, Heir of Sane.

Your sister crossed the threshold.

Now you must follow."

Roman's breath shattered. "Langley…"

The King nodded slowly.

"She embraced her nature.

Will you?"

Roman's hands trembled.

Because the darkness inside him wasn't fighting the King.

It was answering him.

Calling back.

Recognizing him.

James grabbed Roman again, desperate. "Roman, listen to me! You're not whatever this thing says you are. You're my brother. You're a cop. You're a father. You're…."

Roman's voice cracked. "I don't know what I am."

The King stepped closer, shadows swirling around him like a cloak.

"You are ours."

Roman's knees buckled.

Because for the first time in his life…

The darkness didn't feel like an intruder.

It felt like home.

INTERLUDE 1 — WHAT HAPPENED TO LANGLEY

Langley Sane did not die in the alley.

She remembered the bullets, the heat, the impact, the way her body jerked with each shot. She remembered Cage screaming her name. She remembered Kaye firing back blindly. She remembered the pavement rushing up to meet her.

But she did not remember dying.

Because she didn't.

The moment her heart stopped, the world around her dissolved into darkness not the darkness of death, but something deeper. Something alive. Something waiting.

She opened her eyes to a void that stretched infinitely in every direction. No sky. No ground. No horizon. Just blackness that pulsed like a heartbeat.

Her heartbeat.

Langley staggered forward, clutching her chest. "Where the hell am I?"

A voice answered not from the void, but from inside her bones.

"Between."

Langley spun around. "Who's there?"

The darkness shifted, forming a tall, slender, feminine shape. A silhouette made of smoke and shadow. Its eyes glowed faintly, like embers buried under ash.

"You crossed the threshold," the figure said.

"You were chosen long before the bullets touched your skin."

Langley's jaw clenched. "Chosen for what?"

The figure stepped closer, and the void rippled around her like disturbed water.

"To inherit what your bloodline abandoned."

Langley's breath caught. "Bloodline? You mean Roman?"

The figure tilted its head.

"Roman is the Heir.

But you…

you are the Key."

Langley's pulse quickened. "I don't understand."

The figure extended a hand, and the void around them shifted revealing flashes of memory that weren't hers.

A throne of shadows.

A crown of bone.

A war older than humanity.

A child marked at birth.

A girl born second but bound first.

Langley stumbled back. "No. No, that's not me. I'm not part of this."

The figure's voice deepened.

"You always were.

You just didn't know the name of the darkness that raised you."

Langley's breath trembled.

Because she had always felt something like a pull, a whisper, a shadow that followed her through the streets of Baltimore. She thought it was instinct. Trauma. Survival.

But it wasn't.

It was lineage.

The figure stepped closer, its form flickering.

"Your brother hears the voice.

You hear the silence."

Langley frowned. "Silence?"

"The space between worlds.

The place where kings are born

and monsters kneel."

Langley swallowed hard. "Why me?"

The figure's eyes glowed brighter.

"Because you died.

And in dying, you awakened."

Langley's heart pounded. "Awakened into what?"

The void trembled.

A roar echoed through the darkness, the same roar Roman heard miles away in the armory. The sound shook Langley to her knees, vibrating through her skull, her spine, her soul.

The figure whispered:

"The King has risen.

And you…

you are his herald."

Langley's eyes widened in horror. "No. I'm not serving anything. I'm not…"

The figure touched her forehead.

And Langley saw everything.

The King's rise.

The creatures spilling into the world.

Roman standing in the armory, marked by destiny.

The shadow lineage of the Sane bloodline.

The war that was coming.

The throne that waited.

The crown that would not be denied.

Langley screamed.

The void swallowed the sound.

When she opened her eyes again, she was no longer in the between.

She was standing behind the King.

Alive.

Changed.

Reborn.

Her eyes glowed with the same unnatural darkness as Roman's.

And she whispered, with a voice that was no longer entirely her own:

"I'm coming, little brother."

INTERLUDE 2 — LANGLEY WATCHES ROMAN

Langley stood in the ruins of the station long before the King arrived.

Not physically.

Not in flesh.

But in the way shadows gather in corners where light refuses to reach.

She watched Roman fight, watched the way he moved with a precision no human should possess. Watched the way the creatures recoiled from him, not out of fear, but out of recognition.

Her voice, the voice she once used to tease him, to scold him, to protect him, was gone.

Replaced by something colder.

Sharper.

Older.

But her memories remained.

She remembered Roman at six years old, fists clenched, eyes burning with a rage he didn't understand.

She remembered pulling him off Ryan in the alley.

She remembered the pencil in Terrell's leg.

She remembered the voice he heard — the one he never admitted to.

She remembered everything.

And now, standing in the shadows of the armory, she saw the truth she had never seen before:

Roman wasn't hearing the darkness.

He was answering it.

Langley stepped closer, her form flickering like a candle flame in a storm. The officers couldn't see her. James couldn't see her. The King hadn't summoned her yet.

But Roman…

Roman felt her.

His breath hitched. His eyes darted to the corner of the room — the exact spot where Langley stood, half-formed, half-real, half-alive.

He whispered, "Langley…?"

Langley's heart…whatever remained of it — twisted.

She reached out, her hand passing through the air like smoke. Her fingers brushed the edge of Roman's consciousness, and for a moment, she felt him.

His fear.

His confusion.

His anger.

His destiny.

Roman staggered, clutching his head. "No… no, that's not real."

Langley's voice — the new one, the Herald's voice — slipped into his mind like a blade sliding between ribs.

"I'm here, Rome."

Roman froze.

James grabbed his arm. "Roman? Roman, what is it?"

Roman didn't answer.

Because Langley stepped fully into view — not for James, not for the officers, but for Roman alone.

Her eyes glowed with the same abyssal darkness as the King's. Her skin flickered between humans and shadows. Her presence bent the air around her.

But her expression…

Her expression was the same one she wore when they were kids, and she found him bleeding after a fight.

Protective.

Fierce.

Terrified.

Roman whispered, "Langley… what did they do to you?"

Langley shook her head slowly.

"They didn't do this to me."

She stepped closer, her form stabilizing.

"I chose this."

Roman's breath shattered. "Why?"

Langley's voice softened — the only softness left in her.

"To save you."

The King's roar echoed through the station, shaking the walls. Officers screamed. The armory door buckled.

Langley didn't look away from Roman.

"He's coming for you, Rome.

Because you're not just part of this.

You're the center of it."

Roman's eyes widened. "Langley… what am I?"

Langley's form flickered violently, as if something was pulling her back.

She whispered one final truth — the one she wasn't supposed to say.

"You're not becoming like them."

She reached out, her hand passing through his chest, touching something deeper.

"They're becoming like you."

And then she vanished.

The King stepped through the door.

And Roman understood:

He wasn't being hunted.

He was being claimed.

INTERLUDE 3 — LANGLEY'S NEW POWERS

Langley stood in the void after her transformation, her body flickering between flesh and shadow. She felt weightless, unbound, as if gravity no longer recognized her. The darkness around her pulsed like a living thing, responding to her breath, her heartbeat, her thoughts.

She raised her hand.

The shadows rose with it.

Not like smoke.

Not like mist.

But like soldiers obeying a command.

Langley stared at her own fingers — they were still hers, still slender, still marked by the scars of a life lived in Baltimore's streets. But now they shimmered with a faint, dark glow, as if something ancient had been poured into her veins.

A voice…. not the King's, but something older. It whispered through the void.

"You are the Herald.

The one who walks between."

Langley swallowed. "Between what?"

The darkness rippled.

"Between life and death.

Between shadow and flesh.

Between the King and the Heir."

Langley's breath trembled. "Roman…"

The void shifted, revealing a vision — Roman in the armory, surrounded by officers, fear and destiny warring in his eyes. Langley reached toward the image, and the shadows obeyed, stretching forward like tendrils.

Her hand passed through the vision — and she felt him.

His heartbeat.

His confusion.

His rage.

His awakening.

Langley gasped. "I can feel him."

"You are bound," the voice said.

"As all Heralds are bound to their Heirs."

Langley's pulse quickened. "What else can I do?"

The darkness answered not with words, but with revelation.

POWER ONE: SHADOW FORM

Langley's body dissolved into smoke — not disappearing, but becoming something incorporeal, something that could slip through cracks, through walls, through the thin spaces between moments.

She reformed instantly, whole again.

She didn't breathe hard.

She didn't sweat.

She didn't feel pain.

She felt limitless.

POWER TWO: VEIL SIGHT

The void shifted again, showing her the world of the living — but not as humans saw it.

She saw the creatures swarming the city, their bodies wrapped in threads of darkness that pulsed like veins. She saw the King's influence spreading like a storm cloud. She saw the thin places where reality was tearing.

And she saw Roman glowing faintly — not with light, but with a darkness that matched her own.

Langley whispered, "He's marked…"

"He is more than marked," the voice replied.

"He is the center."

POWER THREE: MIND-TOUCH

Langley focused on Roman again.

She didn't speak.

She didn't reach.

She simply thought.

And Roman heard her.

He flinched in the armory, clutching his head, whispering her name.

Langley smiled — not cruelly, but with a fierce, protective love.

"I can reach him," she said. "I can guide him."

"You can influence him," the voice corrected.

"But you cannot control him.

The Heir chooses his own path."

Langley's jaw tightened. "Then I'll make sure he chooses the right one."

POWER FOUR: HERALD'S CALL

The void trembled as Langley felt something stir inside her, a vibration, a resonance, a note in a song she had never heard but somehow knew by heart.

She opened her mouth.

And the darkness answered.

A sound — low, haunting, ancient — rippled through the void and into the world of the living. The creatures outside the station froze, their heads snapping toward the sky.

They heard her.

They obeyed her.

Langley staggered, overwhelmed. "I… I can command them."

"You can command the lesser," the voice said.

"But the King commands you."

Langley's expression hardened. "We'll see about that."

POWER FIVE: THE HERALD'S MEMORY

The final power came not as a gift, but as a burden.

Langley saw flashes of memories not her own.

A war before humanity.

A throne forged from the bones of fallen kings.

A prophecy carved into the fabric of the void.

A bloodline chosen to bridge the world.

A child born with the voice of the dark.

A sister born with the silence of the void.

Langley fell to her knees, clutching her head.

"Why us?" she whispered. "Why the Sane bloodline?"

The voice answered with a truth that chilled her to her core.

"Because your family was never meant to survive the light."

Langley's eyes darkened.

She rose slowly; her new powers settled into her like a second skin.

She looked toward the vision of Roman — terrified, awakening, hunted.

And she whispered:

"I'm coming for you, Rome.

Not to save you.

To prepare you."

The void swallowed her.

And Langley stepped into the world again — not as a sister.

But as the Herald.

INTERLUDE 4 — THE KING REACTS TO THE TRUTH

The King felt her before he saw her.

The void trembled — a subtle shift, like a ripple across still water. The shadows around him recoiled, then leaned forward, as if bowing to a new presence. The King's form flickered, his silhouette warping with irritation.

This was not part of the design.

Her awakening was early.

Unplanned.

Unbidden.

The King turned slowly, his body bending like smoke caught in a storm. His eyes — if they could be called eyes — glowed with cold, ancient intelligence.

Langley stood behind him.

Not fully formed.

Not fully shadow.

Caught between worlds.

Her body flickered, her outline unstable, but her gaze was steady — sharp, defiant, unafraid.

The King studied her.

"You crossed without permission."

Langley smirked — the same smirk she used to give Roman when she beat him at anything.

"Permission?" she said. "I didn't know I needed to ask."

The shadows around the King hissed, recoiling from her insolence. The void itself seemed to tighten, as if bracing for punishment.

But the King did not strike her.

He stepped closer.

"You were not chosen to awaken first."

Langley tilted her head. "Then maybe you should've picked someone else to shoot."

The King's form rippled with irritation.

"Your death was meant to break the Heir.

Not elevate you."

Langley's smile faded.

"Roman isn't breaking," she said. "He's waking up."

The King's voice deepened, vibrating through the void.

"He is awakening because of me.

Not because of you."

Langley stepped forward, her shadow trailing behind her like a living thing.

"No," she said quietly. "He's awakening because he's always been more than you understood."

The King's form twisted violently, the void shaking with his anger.

"You presume too much, Herald."

Langley didn't flinch.

she asked. "Or do you fear that Roman might not kneel as easily as you think?"

The King froze.

For the first time since the dawn of his existence, something like uncertainty flickered across his form.

Langley saw it.

And she smiled.

THE KING TESTS HER

The King extended his hand, and the void around Langley constricted — shadows tightening like a noose, pressing against her form, testing her strength, her will, her allegiance.

Langley gasped as the darkness tried to crush her.

But she didn't break.

She didn't kneel.

She didn't scream.

She pushed back.

Her own shadows surged outward, meeting the King's force with a power she didn't know she possessed. The void trembled, the darkness warping, the air vibrating with the clash of two supernatural wills.

The King withdrew his hand.

Not because she defeated him.

But because she endured.

He studied her again — this time with something new in his gaze.

Not anger.

Not irritation.

Recognition.

"You are stronger than expected."

Langley wiped blood — or something like blood — from her lip.

"Yeah," she said. "I get that a lot."

The King's voice lowered.

"You are not the Heir.

But you are… useful."

Langley's eyes narrowed. "I'm not here to serve you."

The King's form flickered, towering over her.

"You already do."

Langley's jaw clenched. "I serve one person."

The King tilted his head.

"Roman."

Langley didn't deny it.

The King's voice softened — not gentle but calculating.

"Then guide him.

Shape him.

Prepare him."

Langley's breath caught. "For what?"

The King leaned close, his presence suffocating.

"For the throne."

Langley's heart — whatever remained of it — twisted.

"Roman isn't a king," she whispered.

The King's laughter shook the void.

"He is not a king yet."

Langley stepped back, her form flickering with fear and fury.

The King turned away, dismissing her.

"Go to him, Herald.

Watch him.

Whisper to him.

Lead him to me."

Langley hesitated.

Then she vanished into shadow.

Not because she obeyed.

But because she knew the truth:

If she didn't guide Roman…

the King would.

INTERLUDE 5 — ROMAN'S FIRST SURGE

The King stepped through the shattered armory door, and the world seemed to fold inward around him. Officers collapsed under the weight of his presence, their minds buckling as if gravity itself had turned hostile.

James staggered, choking on air that suddenly felt too thick to breathe.

But Roman…

Roman stood perfectly still.

Not because he was brave.

Not because he was strong.

But because something inside him recognized the King — not as an enemy…

…but as a mirror.

The King's form flickered, shadows writhing around him like serpents.

"Heir."

The word hit Roman like a physical blow. His knees buckled, his vision blurred, and a pressure built behind his eyes — sharp, burning, ancient.

James grabbed him. "Roman! Stay with me!"

Roman didn't hear him.

Because the voice inside him — the one that had whispered all his life — wasn't whispering anymore.

It was roaring.

Wake up.

Roman gasped, clutching his chest. His heartbeat thundered, each pulse shaking the air around him. The lights flickered violently. The shadows on the walls twisted into impossible shapes.

James stumbled back. "Roman… your eyes…"

Roman's irises darkened, swirling like ink dropped into water. His veins pulsed with a faint black glow, spreading across his skin like cracks in porcelain.

The King stepped closer.

"Yes.

There it is."

Roman's breath came in ragged bursts. "Get… out… of my head."

The King's laughter shook the room.

"I am not in your head.

I am in your blood."

Roman screamed.

Not in fear.

In awakening.

The surge hit him like a tidal wave — a rush of power so overwhelming it felt like drowning in fire and ice at the same time. His body arched, his hands clawing at the air as shadows erupted from his skin, swirling around him in violent spirals.

Officers crawled away, terrified.

James shielded his face from the blast of dark energy radiating off Roman.

"Roman! Fight it!"

Roman couldn't.

Because the darkness wasn't attacking him.

It was answering him.

Langley appeared in the corner of the room — half-shadow, half-flesh — watching with wide, conflicted eyes.

"Rome… stop. You're not ready."

Roman didn't hear her.

His scream deepened, layered with another voice — older, deeper, inhuman.

The King's eyes gleamed.

"He is ready."

Roman's feet lifted off the ground, shadows coiling around him like chains and wings at the same time. His heartbeat thundered, shaking the walls. The emergency lights shattered, plunging the room into darkness lit only by the glow of Roman's veins.

James whispered, horrified, "Roman… what are you?"

Roman's voice came out distorted — two tones overlapping.

"I don't… know…"

The King extended a hand.

"You are mine."

Roman's surge exploded.

A shockwave of darkness blasted outward, hurling officers across the room, shattering glass, bending metal. The King's shadows recoiled, surprised — not by the power…

…but by the force of it.

Langley stepped forward, eyes wide.

"Rome… you're stronger than him."

Roman collapsed to the floor, gasping, trembling, smoke rising from his skin.

The King stared at him — not with anger.

With hunger.

"Heir of Sane…

your throne awaits."

Roman lifted his head, eyes glowing with a darkness that wasn't the King's.

It was his own.

INTERLUDE 6 — ROMAN RESISTS THE KING

Roman lay on the floor of the armory, chest heaving, shadows still curling off his skin like smoke. The surge had nearly torn him apart — but it had also awakened something inside him.

Something the King did not expect.

The King stepped forward, towering over him, his form flickering between shapes — beast, man, shadow, crown. His presence pressed against the walls, bending the air, warping the light.

"Rise, Heir."

Roman didn't move.

Not because he couldn't.

Because he refused.

The King's voice deepened, vibrating through the floor.

"You are mine."

Roman's fingers dug into the cracked tile. His breath steadied. His eyes — still glowing with that unnatural darkness — lifted to meet the King's.

"No."

The King froze.

Not because the word mattered — but because of the way Roman said it.

Not with fear.

Not with defiance.

With authority.

James stared, stunned. "Roman… what are you doing?"

Roman pushed himself to his knees, shadows swirling around him like a storm trying to form wings.

"I'm not yours," he said, voice layered with something ancient. "I'm not your weapon. I'm not your heir. I'm not your throne."

The King's form rippled violently, the void around him trembling.

"You cannot resist what you are."

Roman stood.

And the shadows obeyed him.

They rose from the floor, from the walls, from the corners of the room — not toward the King, but toward Roman, wrapping around him like armor.

Langley appeared in the corner, half-shadow, half-flesh, eyes wide.

"Rome… stop. You don't know what you're doing."

Roman didn't look at her.

He took a step toward the King.

The King's voice thundered.

"You are bound to me by blood."

Roman's voice thundered back — not louder, but deeper, resonant, carrying the weight of something older than the King himself.

"No.

I'm bound to nothing."

The King recoiled.

For the first time since the dawn of his existence…

he stepped back.

Langley gasped. "Rome… he's afraid of you."

The King's shadows writhed, twisting violently.

"You are not ready."

Roman's eyes darkened further — not with the King's power, but with his own.

"Then you should've killed me when you had the chance."

The King's form flickered, unstable.

"You will kneel."

Roman stepped closer.

"No."

"You will serve."

Roman's shadows surged.

"No."

"You will become—"

Roman cut him off.

"I will become what I choose."

The King roared — a sound that cracked the walls, shattered the remaining lights, and sent officers screaming.

But Roman didn't flinch.

He raised his hand.

And the shadows in the room bent toward him — not the King.

For a moment, the King's form flickered violently, as if the world itself was trying to reject him.

Langley whispered, terrified and awed:

"Rome… you're overriding him."

The King's voice dropped to a low, dangerous growl.

"You are stronger than I anticipated."

Roman's jaw clenched. "Get out of my station."

The King's form twisted, collapsing inward like a dying star.

"This is not over, Heir."

Roman stepped forward, shadows swirling around him like a crown.

"It is for now."

The King vanished — not defeated but forced to retreat.

The room fell silent.

James stared at Roman, trembling. "What… what the hell are you?"

Roman looked down at his hands — still glowing, still trembling, still wrapped in darkness.

"I don't know," he whispered.

Langley stepped from the shadows, her voice soft.

"You're the only thing he's ever feared."

Roman closed his eyes.

And for the first time since the world began to fall apart…

The voice inside him was silent.

AFTER ROMAN RESISTS THE KING

The King vanished, leaving behind a silence so heavy it felt like the air itself was grieving. The armory was wrecked, walls cracked, lights shattered, officers sprawled across the floor in shock.

But none of them looked at the destruction.

They looked at Roman.

He stood in the center of the room, chest rising and falling slowly, shadows still curling around him like smoke that refused to dissipate. His eyes glowed faintly — not with the King's power, but with something deeper.

Something that belonged to him.

James approached cautiously, as if Roman were a bomb that hadn't decided whether to explode.

"Roman… talk to me."

Roman didn't answer.

He was listening.

Not to James.

Not to the officers.

Not even to the silence.

He was listening to the darkness inside him — the one that had whispered all his life, the one that had bowed to the King, the one that had roared during the surge.

But now…

It wasn't whispering.

It wasn't bowing.

It wasn't roaring.

It was waiting.

Roman swallowed hard. "He's not gone."

James stiffened. "The King?"

Roman nodded. "He retreated. That's all."

James exhaled shakily. "Then we need to get out of here. Regroup. Call for backup. Something."

Roman shook his head.

"No. Backup won't help. Guns won't help. Nothing human will help."

James stared at him. "Roman… what are you saying?"

Roman looked at his hands — still trembling, still glowing faintly, still wrapped in shadows that pulsed like veins.

"I'm saying I'm not human anymore."

James grabbed his shoulder. "Don't say that. Don't you dare say that."

Roman's voice cracked. "You saw what I did."

"I saw you survive," James said. "I saw you fight back. I saw you resist that thing. That's not inhuman. That's you."

Roman shook his head slowly.

"You don't understand. I didn't resist him because I'm strong. I resisted him because I'm like him."

James froze.

Roman continued, voice low, haunted.

"When he spoke… something inside me answered. When he reached for me… something inside me reached back. And when I pushed him away…"

He looked up, eyes darkening.

"…it wasn't because I'm brave. It was because I'm dangerous."

James stepped back, the truth hitting him like a blow.

"Roman… what did he do to you?"

Roman's jaw tightened.

"He didn't do anything to me."

He looked toward the corner of the room — the same corner where Langley had appeared moments before.

"I've always been this."

LANGLEY WATCHES

Langley materialized in the shadows, unseen by the officers, unseen by James — but not unseen by Roman.

He felt her before he saw her.

A cold ripple across his spine.

A whisper of familiarity.

A presence that was both comforting and terrifying.

Roman turned his head slightly. "You're still here."

James blinked. "Who are you talking to?"

Roman didn't answer.

Langley stepped forward, her form flickering between flesh and shadow.

"You did good, Rome."

Roman's breath hitched. "Why didn't you tell me?"

Langley's expression softened — the first human expression she'd shown since her transformation.

"Because you weren't ready."

Roman clenched his fists. "I'm still not ready."

Langley shook her head.

"You're more ready than he is."

Roman frowned. "Who?"

Langley's eyes darkened.

"The King."

Roman's stomach twisted. "He's afraid of me."

Langley nodded.

"He should be."

THE OFFICER'S BREAK

One of the officers — a young rookie with shaking hands — finally snapped.

"Major Sane… what the hell is going on? What were those things? What was that thing? And what the hell is wrong with you?"

James stepped forward. "Watch your tone."

"No!" the rookie shouted. "I saw his eyes! I saw the shadows! He's not— he's not—"

Roman turned toward him.

The rookie froze.

Because Roman's eyes — still glowing faintly — locked onto his.

And for a moment, the rookie felt something press against his mind.

Not an attack.

Not a command.

A presence.

Ancient.

Heavy.

Inevitable.

Roman blinked, and the pressure vanished.

"I'm still your Major," he said quietly. "And I'm still in control."

Langley whispered behind him:

"For now."

Roman ignored her.

He turned to James. "We need to move. The King will regroup. And when he comes back, he won't come alone."

James nodded. "Where do we go?"

Roman looked toward the shattered doorway — toward the burning city beyond it.

"Home," he said. "We start at home."

Langley's voice slid into his mind like a blade.

"Good.

Because that's where the truth is."

Roman stiffened.

"What truth?"

Langley smiled — a dark, knowing smile.

"The truth about us."

ROMAN AND JAMES ESCAPE THE STATION

The station groaned like a dying animal.

Cracks spiderwebbed across the ceiling. Dust drifted down in soft, choking clouds. Somewhere deep in the building, something collapsed with a thunderous crash that shook the floor beneath their feet.

James grabbed Roman's arm. "We need to move. Now."

Roman didn't argue.

He felt the King's retreat like a cold wind pulling away from his skin — not gone, just distant, regrouping, watching. The shadows around Roman still pulsed faintly, responding to his heartbeat, waiting for his command.

He didn't trust them.

He didn't trust himself.

"Everyone up!" James shouted. "We're evacuating!"

Officers staggered to their feet, some limping, some bleeding, all terrified. Their eyes kept darting to Roman — not with hatred, not with suspicion…

With awe.

With fear.

With the knowledge that he was no longer one of them.

Roman ignored their stares.

He focused on the hallway ahead — dark, debris-strewn, flickering with dying lights. The air smelled like smoke and something else… something metallic and ancient.

Langley's voice slid into his mind like a whisper under his skin.

"They're coming back, Rome. Move."

Roman clenched his jaw. "I know."

James glanced at him. "Who are you talking to?"

Roman didn't answer.

THE HALLWAY

They moved fast — Roman in front, James beside him, officers behind them in a tight formation. Every step echoed through the ruined station, every sound amplified by the tension coiling in the air.

Roman's senses were sharper than they'd ever been.

He could hear the heartbeat of every officer behind him.

He could smell the smoke from three rooms away.

He could feel the shadows shifting, whispering, waiting.

James noticed the way Roman's eyes darted, the way his muscles were tense.

"You good?"

Roman shook his head. "No. But I'm moving."

A distant shriek echoed through the station — one of the creatures, but changed, angrier, more desperate.

James flinched. "They're regrouping."

Roman nodded. "The King's calling them."

Langley's voice whispered:

"He's calling you too."

Roman ignored her.

THE STAIRWELL

They reached the stairwell door. Roman pushed it open and froze.

The stairwell was filled with shadows.

Not darkness.

Shadows.

They moved like a living thing, swirling slowly, pulsing with a rhythm that matched Roman's heartbeat.

James whispered, "Roman… what is that?"

Roman swallowed hard. "It's reacting to me."

Langley appeared beside him — unseen by the others, her form flickering like a glitch.

"You can push it back," she said.

"Or you can use it."

Roman's breath hitched. "I don't want to use it."

Langley's eyes softened.

"You won't have a choice."

The shadows surged forward.

Officers screamed.

James raised his weapon.

Roman stepped in front of him.

"STOP!"

The shadows froze.

The officers stared, widely eyed.

James whispered, "Roman… what did you just do?"

Roman didn't know.

He raised his hand slowly.

The shadows recoiled.

Not from fear.

From obedience.

Roman exhaled shakily. "Go. Move. I'll hold it."

James hesitated. "Roman—"

"MOVE!"

James nodded and led the officers down the stairs.

Roman followed last, the shadows parting around him like a tide.

THE EXIT

They burst through the back door into the alley behind the station. Smoke filled the sky. Sirens wailed in the distance. The city was burning.

James doubled over, catching his breath. "We made it."

Roman didn't respond.

Because he felt something behind him.

He turned.

The shadows in the doorway twisted, forming a tall, slender, familiar shape.

Langley.

She stepped into the alley, her form stabilizing in the dim light.

James didn't see her.

But Roman did.

"Langley…"

She smiled — sad, proud, terrified.

"You're changing, Rome."

Roman's voice cracked. "I don't want this."

Langley stepped closer.

"Want has nothing to do with it."

Roman clenched his fists. "I'm not him. I'm not the King."

Langley nodded.

"No.

You're worse."

Roman froze.

Langley's voice softened.

"And that's why he fears you."

Roman looked back at the burning station.

Then at James.

Then at the city.

Then at his sister — half shadow, half memory, half prophecy.

"What do I do now?"

Langley's answer was simple.

"You go home."

Roman swallowed. "And then?"

Langley's eyes darkened.

"Then you learn what you are."

THE ROAD HOME

The alley behind the station was choked with smoke, ash drifting through the air like black snow. The city beyond it burned in patches — buildings half-collapsed, cars overturned, sirens wailing in the distance like dying animals.

Roman stepped into the open, the shadows around him thinning but not disappearing. They clung to him like a second skin, pulsing faintly with each heartbeat.

James followed close behind, weapon drawn, eyes scanning every rooftop and alleyway.

"Roman… where are we going?"

Roman didn't answer immediately.

Because he didn't know.

Not logically.

Not tactically.

Not in any way a police officer should.

He knew because something inside him pulled — a tug in his chest, a whisper in his bones, a direction that felt older than instinct.

"Home," Roman finally said. "We start at home."

James frowned. "Your mother's house? Roman, that place was hit. Hard."

Roman's jaw tightened. "Exactly."

Langley's voice slid into his mind like a cold finger tracing his spine.

"He's not done with that house, Rome.

He left something there."

Roman stiffened.

James noticed. "You okay?"

"No."

He wasn't.

Because the pull in his chest grew stronger — a magnetic force dragging him toward the place where Langley died… and didn't die.

THE WALK THROUGH THE RUINS

They moved through the streets cautiously, officers flanking them, weapons raised. The city felt wrong — too quiet, too still, like the air was holding its breath.

Roman's senses were heightened.

He could hear distant footsteps blocks away.

He could smell blood under the smoke.

He could feel the shadows watching him.

James whispered, "Roman… you're hearing things, aren't you?"

Roman nodded. "Everything."

James swallowed. "Is that… good?"

Roman didn't answer.

Because he didn't know.

Langley appeared beside him — unseen by the others, her form flickering like a glitch.

"You're syncing," she said.

"Your senses are aligning with the Rift."

Roman clenched his fists. "I don't want this."

Langley's expression softened.

"You don't get to want or not want it.

You get to survive it."

Roman's breath hitched.

James glanced at him. "Roman… who are you talking to?"

Roman didn't answer.

THE FIRST SIGN

They turned a corner — and froze.

The street ahead was lined with bodies.

Not human.

Not creature.

Something in between.

Twisted forms, half-shadow, half-flesh, their bodies contorted as if they'd been torn apart from the inside. Their eyes were hollow; their mouths open in silent screams.

James whispered, "Jesus Christ…"

Roman stepped forward slowly.

The shadows around him stirred.

Langley appeared beside one of the bodies, crouching.

"These weren't killed by the King," she said.

"These were killed by you."

Roman's stomach dropped. "No. I didn't—"

Langley shook her head.

"Not on purpose.

Not consciously.

But when you surged… your power rippled through the city."

Roman staggered back. "I killed them?"

Langley stood.

"You unmade them."

James looked at Roman, horrified. "Roman… what is she saying?"

Roman didn't answer.

Because he couldn't.

THE PULL INTENSIFIES

The tug in Roman's chest grew stronger — painful now, like a hook lodged in his heart.

He gasped, clutching his chest.

James grabbed him. "Roman! What's happening?"

Roman's voice cracked. "He's calling me."

Langley stepped closer, her voice urgent.

"Not the King.

Something else.

Something older."

Roman's eyes widened. "Older?"

Langley nodded.

"The truth.

The origin.

The reason our bloodline exists."

Roman's breath trembled.

James looked between them, confused and terrified. "Roman… what truth?"

Roman looked toward the horizon — toward his mother's house.

"It's waiting for me."

Langley whispered:

"It always has."

CHAPTER 7 — THE HOUSE OF THE SANES

The deeper they moved into the city, the quieter it became.

Not peaceful quiet.

Predatory quiet.

The kind of silence that feels like something is listening.

Roman walked ahead of the group, his steps steady but his pulse hammering. The shadows around him thinned with distance from the station, but they didn't disappear. They clung to him like a scent the world could smell.

James kept pace beside him, glancing at Roman every few seconds as if expecting him to collapse… or explode.

"Roman," James said softly, "you don't have to do this alone."

Roman didn't look at him. "I'm not alone."

James frowned. "You mean the officers?"

Roman shook his head.

Langley walked beside him. She was unseen by everyone but him — her form flickering like a candle flame in a draft.

"He means me," she said.

Roman clenched his jaw. "I didn't ask for you."

Langley smirked. "You never had to."

James watched Roman's expression shift, confused. "You're hearing her again, aren't you."

Roman didn't answer.

Because the pull in his chest grew stronger — a magnetic force dragged him toward the house he grew up in. Toward the place where Langley died. Toward the place where the King first touched their bloodline.

Langley's voice slid into his mind.

"You're close."

Roman swallowed. "I know."

THE NEIGHBORHOOD

They turned onto Roman's childhood street. It was unrecognizable. Houses were burned; cars were smoldered. There were bodies, both humans and creatures lay twisted in the road, but the strangest part wasn't the destruction.

It was the absence.

No movement.

No sound.

No creatures.

James whispered, "Where the hell is everybody."

Roman didn't answer.

Because he felt it.

A pressure in the air.

A weight on his chest.

A presence waiting.

Langley stepped ahead of him, her form stabilizing as they approached the house.

"He cleared this street," she said.

"He wanted you to walk it alone."

Roman's breath hitched. "Why."

Langley turned to him, her eyes dark.

"Because this is where it started."

THE HOUSE OF THE SANES

Roman's mother's house stood at the end of the street — half-collapsed, windows shattered, the front door hanging off its hinges.

But the house wasn't dead.

It pulsed.

A faint, rhythmic thrum — like a heartbeat — echoed from within the walls.

James felt it too. "Roman… what is that."

Roman stepped forward.

"It's calling me."

Langley appeared at the doorway, her expression tight.

"Rome… listen to me."

Roman froze.

Langley never sounded afraid.

"Whatever's inside… it's not just the King."

Roman's stomach twisted. "Then what is it."

Langley hesitated.

And that terrified him more than anything.

"It's the thing he serves."

Roman's blood ran cold.

James grabbed his arm. "Roman. Stop. We regroup. We think. We don't walk into—"

Roman pulled away.

"I have to."

James stepped in front of him. "Why."

Roman looked at the house — at the place where he grew up, where he fought, where he bled, where he first heard the voice.

"Because this house has been lying to me my whole life."

Langley nodded slowly.

"And it's time it told the truth."

Roman stepped toward the doorway.

The heartbeat inside the house grew louder.

James whispered, "Roman… don't go in there."

Roman didn't look back.

"I don't have a choice."

Langley's voice followed him like a shadow.

"No, Rome.

You have a destiny."

Roman crossed the threshold.

And the door shut behind him.

THE FIRST MEMORY RETURNS

The door shut behind Roman with a force that rattled the entire house. Dust drifted from the ceiling. The heartbeat pulsing through the walls grew louder, deeper, older.

Roman froze.

Because the moment he stepped inside, something pressed against his mind — not a voice, not a whisper, but a weight. Heavy. Familiar. Ancient.

Langley appeared beside him, her form flickering like a dying bulb.

"Rome… brace yourself."

Roman swallowed. "For what."

Langley didn't answer.

Because the house did.

The walls shuddered.

The floorboards groaned.

The air thickened until it felt like breathing through wet cloth.

And then—

A sound.

Soft.

High.

Childlike.

A boy crying.

Roman's breath hitched. "No… no, that's not real."

Langley's voice softened.

"It is."

The sound grew louder — a child sobbing, gasping, choking on fear. Roman staggered forward, clutching his head as the memory clawed its way up from the depths of his mind.

The house around him dissolved.

The present peeled away.

And Roman was six years old again.

THE MEMORY

He stood in the hallway of the same house — but younger, smaller, trembling. The wallpaper was new. The lights were bright. The air smelled like his mother's perfume.

And he was crying.

Not from pain.

Not from fear.

From something inside him.

A shadow curled around his feet — small, thin, like smoke rising from a candle. It pulsed with his heartbeat.

Little Roman sobbed harder. "Stop… stop… please stop…"

A voice — the first voice — whispered inside his skull.

Wake up.

Little Roman screamed.

The shadow surged upward, wrapping around his arms, his chest, his throat. His eyes rolled back. His body convulsed.

He wasn't being attacked.

He was awakening.

The hallway lights flickered violently. The shadows on the walls twisted into impossible shapes. The air vibrated with a low, ancient hum.

And then—

A door burst open.

Langley — twelve years old — sprinted into the hallway, eyes wide with terror.

"Roman!"

She grabbed him, shaking him, trying to pull him out of the shadows.

But the shadows weren't attacking him.

They were coming from him.

Little Roman screamed again, and the shadows exploded outward — a shockwave that shattered the hallway mirror, cracked the walls, and sent Langley flying backward.

She hit the floor hard, gasping.

"Rome… stop! Please stop!"

But he couldn't.

Because the voice inside him whispered again.

You are mine.

Little Roman's eyes snapped open — glowing with the same darkness he carried now.

Langley crawled toward him, tears streaming down her face.

"Rome… please… come back…"

And then—

Their mother appeared at the end of the hallway.

She froze.

Her face went pale.

Not with fear.

With recognition.

"Not again," she whispered. "God… not again…"

She rushed forward, grabbed Roman, and held him tight — not to comfort him, but to contain him.

"Breathe, baby. Breathe. Don't let it take you."

Little Roman sobbed into her shoulder.

The shadows receded.

The lights steadily.

The voice went silent.

And the memory ended.

BACK IN THE PRESENT

Roman collapsed to his knees, gasping, shaking, sweat dripping down his face.

Langley knelt beside him, her voice soft.

"You remember now."

Roman's voice cracked. "Why… why did she say, 'not again'."

Langley looked away.

"Because you weren't the first."

Roman's blood ran cold.

"Who was."

Langley met his eyes.

"Dad."

INTERLUDE 7 — THE ORIGIN OF THE SANE BLOODLINE

The house pulsed again — a deep, resonant thrum that vibrated through Roman's bones. The walls around him flickered, peeling back like layers of old paint.

Langley stood beside him, her form steady as the truth approached.

"Rome… this is going to hurt."

Roman clenched his jaw. "Do it."

The house was obeyed.

The floor dissolved beneath him.

The walls melted into shadows.

The air thickened until it felt like he was drowning in ink.

And then—

He wasn't in the house anymore.

He was in the Before.

THE BEFORE

There was no sky.

No ground.

No time.

Only a vast, endless expanse of darkness — not empty, but alive. A sea of shadow that pulsed like a living organism.

In the center of it stood a throne.

Not a structure.

A wound.

A tear shaped like a seat, bleeding darkness into the void.

And kneeling before it—

A man.

Tall.

Broad-shouldered.

Head bowed.

Hands trembling.

Roman's breath caught.

"Dad…"

Langley appeared beside him, her voice barely a whisper.

"This is the truth Mom tried to bury."

Roman stepped closer.

His father — Marcus Sane — lifted his head.

His eyes glowed with the same darkness Roman carried now.

But his expression…

His expression was broken.

"I didn't want this," Marcus whispered to the throne.

"I didn't ask to be chosen."

A voice answered — the King's voice, but younger, sharper, less patient.

"You were not chosen.

You were born."

Marcus flinched. "I'm human."

The darkness laughed.

"You are a vessel.

A bridge.

A fracture in the world wearing human skin."

Roman's stomach twisted.

Langley whispered:

"He was the first Sane to awaken."

Marcus clenched his fists.

"I won't serve you."

The darkness rippled.

"You already do."

Marcus screamed as shadows surged into him — not attacking, but entering, filling him, twisting him, rewriting him.

Roman staggered back. "Stop— STOP!"

But the memory didn't stop.

It deepened.

THE FIRST HEIR

Marcus collapsed to the ground, gasping, shaking, his body flickering between flesh and shadow.

The King stepped forward — not the monstrous form Roman knew, but a more human silhouette, tall and regal, crowned in darkness.

"Rise, First Heir."

Marcus didn't rise.

He crawled.

He begged.

"Please… please… not my children. Not them."

The King tilted his head.

"Your bloodline is the doorway.

Your children are the keys."

Roman's heart shattered.

Langley's voice trembled.

"He tried to stop it, Rome.

He tried to break the bloodline."

Marcus slammed his fists into the ground.

"I won't let you take them!"

The King's voice dropped to a whisper that shook the void.

"You cannot stop what you are."

Marcus screamed again — a sound of pure agony — as the darkness inside him surged, consuming him from within.

And then—

The memory shifted.

THE BIRTHRIGHT

Roman saw his mother — younger, terrified — holding a newborn baby.

Him.

His eyes were open.

Glowing.

His mother sobbed. "No… no, not again…"

Marcus stumbled into the room, half-shadow, half-man.

He looked at his son.

And he broke.

"Roman… I'm so sorry."

The King's voice echoed through the memory.

"The Sane bloodline is not cursed.

It is chosen."

Roman whispered, "Chosen for what."

The darkness answered.

"To open the Rift."

BACK IN THE PRESENT

Roman collapsed to the floor of the house, gasping, shaking, tears streaming down his face.

Langley knelt beside him.

"Now you know."

Roman's voice cracked. "Dad… he wasn't a monster."

Langley shook her head.

"No.

He was the first victim."

Roman clenched his fists.

"And I'm the next."

Langley's eyes darkened.

"No, Rome.

You're the last."

Roman looked up, breath trembling.

"What does that mean."

Langley whispered:

"It means the bloodline ends with you.

One way or another."

INTERLUDE VIII — The King's Reaction

The moment Roman's memory snapped back into place, the void trembled.

Not the house.

Not the city.

The void.

The space between worlds.

The place where the King ruled.

The place where the throne bled darkness into eternity.

The King felt it was like a blade sliding between ribs.

A shift.

A crack.

A violation.

Roman had seen the Before.

The King's form flickered violently, shadows writhing around him like serpents in a storm. His silhouette twisted, losing shape, losing control.

"No."

The word echoed through the void, shaking the darkness itself.

"He was not meant to see."

The shadows recoiled from him — not out of obedience, but out of fear. The King's presence warped, destabilizing, as if the truth Roman witnessed had infected the void itself.

He staggered — the King, the ancient one, the devourer of worlds — staggered.

"The memory was sealed."

His voice cracked like thunder.

"The bloodline was bound."

The throne pulled behind him — a wound in reality, bleeding shadow.

The King turned toward it, his form trembling.

"He was not ready."

The throne answered with silence.

The King roared.

"HE WAS NOT READY!"

The void rippled outward in shockwaves, tearing through the darkness like cracks in glass.

THE KING SEES ROMAN

The King extended his hand, and the void parted — revealing Roman inside the house, on his knees, shaking, gasping, remembering.

The King's form twisted with fury.

"You dare look upon what was forbidden."

Roman didn't hear him.

But the King felt Roman's heartbeat.

Strong.

Defiant.

Awakened.

The King's voice dropped to a whisper that could shatter mountains.

"You are becoming too quickly."

The shadows around him hissed.

"You are remembering too much."

His form flickered again — not with power, but with something far more dangerous.

Uncertainty.

"You are not meant to know what you are."

The void pulsed.

The King's voice deepened.

"You are not meant to know what I am."

THE KING'S FEAR

For the first time in his existence, the King felt something he had never felt before.

Not anger.

Not hunger.

Not triumphing.

Fear.

Because Roman had seen the truth.

Because Roman had seen Marcus kneel.

Because Roman had seen the throne.

Because Roman had seen the Before.

Because Roman had seen the thing the King served.

The King's voice cracked.

"He is not ready to know the origin."

The throne pulsed again.

The King recoiled.

"He is not ready to know the end."

THE KING DECIDES

The King straightened, his form stabilizing, his shadows tightening around him like armor.

His voice became cold.

Calculating.

Deadly.

"If he knows the truth…"

The void darkened.

"…then he must be shaped."

The shadows were writhed.

"…or broken."

The King stepped toward the tear, his form dissolving into pure darkness.

"Heir of Sane…"

His voice echoed across worlds.

"…you will kneel."

And the void swallowed him whole.

INTERLUDE IX — THE KING COMES FOR ROMAN

The void split open.

Not gently.

Not with ceremony.

With violence.

A jagged tear ripped through the darkness, spilling shadow-like blood. The King stepped through it, his form unstable, flickering between shapes — horned beast, crowned silhouette, shifting mass of eyes and teeth.

He was unraveling.

Because Roman knew the truth.

Because Roman had seen the Before.

Because Roman had seen the throne.

The King's voice cracked the void.

"He must be stopped."

The shadows recoiled.

Not from the command.

From the fear beneath it.

The King extended a hand, and the void bent around him, forming a path — a corridor of writhing darkness leading toward the world of flesh.

"Heir of Sane…"

His voice deepened, vibrating through realities.

"…you have seen what was forbidden."

The throne pulsed behind him — a slow, ominous heartbeat.

The King turned toward it.

"If he remembers the origin…"

The throne answered with silence.

The King's form twisted.

"…he will remember the end."

He stepped forward.

THE DESCENT

The King tore through the veil between worlds, ripping it open with his bare hands. The tear screamed — a sound like metal bending, like bones breaking, like the world protesting.

He didn't care.

He forced his way through.

The sky above the city darkened instantly, clouds swirling into a vortex of shadow. The air thickened. The temperature dropped. Windows shattered from the pressure.

People screamed.

Creatures fled.

Even the lesser horrors — the ones born from the Rift — scattered like insects.

Because the King was coming.

And he was getting angry.

THE KING ENGAGES ROMAN

He appeared above the street — a towering silhouette of shifting darkness, his presence bending the world around him. Cars buckled. Streetlights bent. Asphalt cracked beneath his weight.

And then he saw him.

Roman.

Inside the house.

On his knees.

Remember.

The King's form convulsed with fury.

"You dare look upon the Before."

Roman didn't hear him.

But the King felt Roman's heartbeat.

Stronger.

Steadier.

Awakened.

The King's voice dropped to a whisper that could kill gods.

"You are becoming too quickly."

The shadows around him were writhed.

"You are remembering too much."

His form flickered again — not with power, but with something far more dangerous.

Uncertainty.

"You are not meant to know what you are."

The void pulsed.

The King's voice deepened.

"You are not meant to know what I am."

THE KING APPROACHES THE HOUSE

He descended slowly, each step cracking the earth. The house trembled. The windows shattered inward. The walls groaned under the weight of his presence.

James and the officers outside screamed, stumbling backward as the King's shadow fell over them.

James raised his weapon — hands shaking.

"Roman! ROMAN!"

The King ignored him.

He reached the front door.

Placed a hand on it.

And whispered:

"Open."

The door disintegrated into dust.

Inside the House

Roman lifted his head.

His eyes glowed.

Not with fear.

With recognition.

Langley appeared beside him, her form flickering violently.

“Rome… he’s here.”

Roman stood slowly.

“I know.”

Langley grabbed his arm — her hand passing through him like smoke.

“You can’t fight him yet.”

Roman clenched his fists.

“I’m not fighting him.”

Langley froze.

“Then what are you doing.”

Roman looked toward the doorway — toward the King’s silhouette filling the frame like a living eclipse.

“I’m ending this.”

THE KING ENTERS

The King stepped inside.

The house bowed around him — walls bending, floorboards cracking, shadows crawling toward him like worshippers.

He looked at Roman.

Not with hunger.

Not with triumph.

With rage.

"You were not meant to see the throne."

Roman's voice was steady.

"I saw it anyway."

The King's form twisted violently.

"You were not meant to know the origin."

Roman stepped forward.

"I know it anyway."

The King roared — a sound that shook the entire block.

"YOU WERE NOT MEANT TO REMEMBER!"

Roman's eyes darkened.

"I remember anyway."

The King lunged.

And the house exploded into darkness.

CHAPTER 8 — The First Clash

The house didn't explode outward.

It imploded.

Walls folded like paper.

Floorboards curled upward.

The ceiling bent as if gravity reversed.

Roman stood in the center of it all, shadows swirling around him like a storm trying to form a spine.

The King stepped through the collapsing doorway — a towering silhouette of shifting darkness, his presence bending the world around him.

James and the officers outside screamed as the King's shadow swallowed the porch.

Langley appeared beside Roman, her form flickering violently.

"Rome… brace yourself."

Roman didn't move.

He stared at the King.

And the King stared back.

Not with hunger.

Not with triumph.

With rage.

"You were not meant to remember."

Roman's voice was steady.

"I remember anyway."

The King's form twisted violently, shadows writhing like serpents.

"You were not meant to see the throne."

Roman stepped forward.

"I saw it anyway."

The King roared — a sound that cracked the walls and shook the entire block.

"YOU WERE NOT MEANT TO KNOW THE ORIGIN!"

Roman's eyes darkened.

"I know it anyway."

The King lunged.

THE IMPACT

The King's hand — a mass of shadow and bone — slammed into Roman's chest.

Roman flew backward, crashing through what remained of the living room wall. Dust exploded around him. The floor cracked beneath his body.

James screamed from outside. "ROMAN!"

Roman pushed himself up slowly.

The King stepped into the room, each footfall cracking the floor.

"You are not ready."

Roman wiped blood from his lip.

"Then you should've killed me when you had the chance."

The King's form convulsed.

"You are not strong enough to resist me."

Roman stood.

And the shadows obeyed him.

They rose from the floor, from the walls, from the corners of the room — not toward the King, but toward Roman, wrapping around him like armor.

Langley gasped.

"Rome… you're syncing with the Rift."

Roman didn't hear her.

He stepped forward.

The King swung again — a massive, crushing blow.

Roman caught it.

With one hand.

The King froze.

Because Roman didn't just block the strike.

He absorbed it.

The shadows around Roman pulsed, feeding on the King's power, drinking it like oxygen.

Roman's voice dropped to a low, dangerous growl.

"You don't get to decide what I become."

The King recoiled.

For the first time since the dawn of his existence…

He stepped back.

THE KING'S DESPERATION

The King's form flickered violently, losing shape, losing control.

"You are becoming too quickly."

Roman stepped closer.

"You're afraid."

The King roared.

"I FEAR NOTHING!"

Roman's eyes glowed.

"You fear me."

The King lunged again — faster, harder, desperate.

Roman didn't block.

He didn't dodge.

He surged.

A shockwave of darkness exploded from his body, hurling the King backward through the hallway. The walls shattered. The floor split. The house groaned under the force.

Langley shielded her face, her form flickering.

"Rome… stop! You're not ready!"

Roman didn't stop.

He walked toward the King slowly, steady, inevitable.

The King struggled to rise, his form glitching like a corrupted shadow.

Roman stood over him.

"You wanted an heir."

The King hissed.

"You are not the heir."

Roman leaned in.

"No."

His voice deepened — layered, ancient, resonant.

"I'm the end."

The King's form convulsed.

"You cannot end what you do not understand."

Roman's eyes darkened further.

"Then teach me."

The King screamed — a sound that tore through the house, through the street, through the city.

And the world went black.

CHAPTER 9 — The Blackout

There was no sound.

No light.

No air.

No world.

Just black.

A perfect, suffocating void.

Roman floated in it — weightless, breathless, suspended in a darkness that felt alive. The shadows didn't cling to him anymore.

They held him.

Cradled him.

Studied him.

Langley's voice echoed somewhere far away, muffled, distorted.

"Rome… stay with me…"

But Roman couldn't move.

Couldn't speak.

Couldn't breathe.

Because the blackout wasn't just darkness.

It was the Rift.

The space between worlds.

The place where the King was born.

The place where the Sane bloodline was forged.

And now Roman was inside it.

THE RIFT SPEAKS

A low hum vibrated through the void — not sound, but sensation. It pulsed through Roman's bones, through his blood, through the shadows wrapped around him.

Then a voice — not the King's — whispered:

"Heir…"

Roman's eyes snapped open.

He wasn't floating anymore.

He was falling.

Through darkness.

Through memory.

Through time.

The voice followed him.

"You have awakened."

Roman gasped, trying to breathe, but the Rift didn't have air.

It was true.

"You have seen the Before."

Images flashed around him — his father kneeling, the throne bleeding darkness, the King rising from the void.

"You have seen the origin."

More images — his mother holding him as a newborn, his eyes glowing, the shadows curling around his crib.

"Now you must see the end."

Roman screamed as the darkness swallowed him whole.

OUTSIDE THE BLACKOUT

James stumbled backward as the house collapsed inward, swallowed by a sphere of pure shadow. Officers screamed, firing useless rounds into the darkness.

The King's silhouette flickered inside the sphere — massive, unstable, thrashing like a trapped animal.

James shouted, "ROMAN! ROMAN!"

But the darkness didn't answer.

Langley appeared beside him — fully formed, her eyes wide with terror.

James raised his weapon. "Stay back!"

Langley didn't even look at him.

"He's inside the Rift."

James blinked. "What the hell does that mean."

Langley swallowed hard.

"It means he's not fighting the King anymore."

James stepped closer to the sphere.

"Then what is he fighting."

Langley whispered:

"Himself."

BACK IN THE RIFT

Roman hit something solid a floor made of shadow, a surface that rippled like water but held like stone.

He staggered to his feet.

The darkness around him shifted.

And the King appeared.

Not the towering monster.

Not the crowned silhouette.

Not the devourer of worlds.

A man.

Tall.

Broad-shouldered.

Eyes black as ink.

He looked like Marcus.

Roman's breath caught. "No… no, that's not real."

The King smiled — a human smile stretched too wide.

"You wanted truth."

Roman stepped back.

The King stepped forward.

"Here it is."

Roman clenched his fists. "Get out of my head."

The King shook his head slowly.

"This is not your head."

He spread his arms.

The Rift pulsed.

"This is your inheritance."

Roman's heart pounded.

The King's voice deepened.

"And now that you know the truth…"

He leaned in.

"…you must choose."

Roman swallowed. "Choose what."

The King whispered:

"What kind of god you will become."

CHAPTER 10 — In the Rift: The Choice thc King Fears

Roman stood in the endless dark, the Rift pulsing around him like a living heartbeat. The King wearing Marcus's face, wearing a lie — circled him slowly.

Not attacking.

Not roaring.

Not commanding.

Studying.

"You are accelerating," the King said, voice echoing through the void.

"Faster than any Sane before you."

Roman's jaw tightened. "I'm not like them."

The King smiled — a thin, unnatural stretch of lips.

"No.

You are worse."

Roman stepped back.

The King stepped forward.

"You saw the throne.

You saw the Before.

You saw the truth of your father."

Roman's breath hitched. "He tried to stop you."

The King's smile vanished.

"He failed."

Roman's fists clenched. "I won't."

The King's form flickered, shadows writhing like serpents.

"You misunderstand, Heir."

He leaned in, his voice dropping to a whisper that vibrated through Roman's bones.

"You cannot stop me…

because you are me."

Roman's heart slammed against his ribs.

"No."

The King's eyes darkened.

"Your bloodline was forged from my shadow."

Roman shook his head. "You're lying."

The King spread his arms.

The Rift pulsed.

"You felt it when you surged.

You felt it when you resisted me.

You felt it when you remembered."

Roman staggered.

Because he had felt it.

The King stepped closer.

"You are not my heir."

Roman froze.

The King whispered:

"You are my replacement."

THE RIFT REACTS

The darkness around them convulsed — rippling like a storm-tossed sea. Roman felt something inside him respond, something ancient, something hungry.

Langley's voice echoed faintly from the edge of the void.

"Rome… don't listen to him…"

But the King drowned her out.

"The throne does not choose kings."

He pointed at Roman.

"It chooses endings."

Roman's breath trembled. "What does that mean."

The King's voice cracked like thunder.

"It means the Sane bloodline was created to kill me."

Roman staggered backward.

The King advanced.

"You are not meant to serve."

Another step.

"You are meant to replace."

Another.

"You are meant to devour."

Roman's pulse roared in his ears.

"No… no, that's not—"

The King's voice became a roar that shook the Rift.

"YOU ARE MEANT TO END ME!"

The darkness exploded outward.

ROMAN AWAKENS

Roman fell to his knees, clutching his head as memories — not his own — flooded him.

Kings before the King.

Bloodlines before the Sane.

Thrones before the Rift.

Each one ending the last.

Each one devouring the one before it.

Each one becomes the new King.

Roman screamed.

The King watched.

Not triumphant.

Terrified.

"You were not meant to know this yet."

Roman's eyes snapped open.

They glowed with a darkness that wasn't the King's.

It was older.

Deeper.

Hungrier.

Roman stood.

The Rift trembled.

The King stepped back.

"No… no, this is too soon…"

Roman's voice was layered — human and inhuman, young and ancient.

"I'm not your heir."

The King shook his head violently.

"STOP—"

Roman stepped forward.

"I'm your end."

OUTSIDE THE RIFT

James watched the sphere of darkness crack like an egg.

Langley appeared beside him, eyes wide with horror.

James whispered, "What's happening."

Langley swallowed.

"Roman isn't fighting the King anymore."

James looked at her. "Then what is he doing."

Langley whispered:

"He's taking his place."

CHAPTER 11 — The Rift Breaks Around Roman

The Rift convulsed.

Not like a storm.

Not like a quake.

Like a living thing in pain.

Roman stood in the center of it, shadows spiraling around him in slow, deliberate coils. His eyes glowed with a darkness that wasn't the King's — deeper, older, hungrier.

The King staggered backward, his form glitching like corrupted code.

"This is too soon…"

Roman took a step forward.

The Rift bent around him.

"You were not meant to awaken this quickly."

Roman's voice was layered — human and inhuman, young and ancient.

"I didn't ask your permission."

The King roared, shadows exploding outward.

"YOU WERE NOT MEANT TO KNOW!"

Roman didn't flinch.

"You should've hidden it better."

THE RIFT SHOWS ITS TEETH

The darkness around them twisted violently, forming shapes — not creatures, not memories, but possibilities.

Roman saw flashes:

- Himself crowned in shadow
- Himself devouring the King
- Himself tearing the Rift open
- Himself closing it forever
- Himself becoming something the world could not survive

The King saw the same visions.

And he panicked.

"STOP! STOP LOOKING!"

Roman stepped closer.

"I'm not looking."

He raised his hand.

"I'm remembering."

The Rift pulsed — a deep, resonant thrum that shook the void.

The King's form convulsed.

"You are not ready to see your end!"

Roman's voice dropped to a whisper that cut through the darkness.

"I'm not seeing my end."

He leaned in.

"I'm seeing yours."

THE KING ATTACKS

The King lunged — not with claws, not with shadow, but with desperation.

He slammed into Roman, trying to force him back, trying to smother the awakening before it completed.

The Rift reacted violently.

Shadows surged.

The void screamed.

Reality bent.

Roman staggered — but didn't fall.

The King struck again.

Roman absorbed it.

The King struck harder.

Roman absorbed that too.

The King's voice cracked.

"WHY ARE YOU NOT BREAKING?"

Roman's eyes glowed brighter.

"Because I'm not your heir."

The King froze.

Roman stepped forward.

"I'm your replacement."

THE RIFT CROWNS HIM

A ring of shadow formed above Roman's head — not a crown, not yet, but the shape of one.

The King recoiled.

"NO. NO, YOU CANNOT—"

Roman's voice deepened.

"You said the throne chooses endings."

The Rift pulsed.

"And I choose yours."

The King screamed — a sound that tore through the void, through the house, through the city.

Outside, James fell to his knees, clutching his ears.

Langley stared at the collapsing sphere of darkness, her voice trembling.

"Rome… stop… you don't know what you're becoming…"

But Roman didn't stop.

He stepped toward the King.

And the Rift bent to him.

THE KING BREAKS

The King's form shattered — not destroyed, but exposed.

Beneath the shifting shadows, beneath the monstrous silhouette, beneath the ancient power…

Was a man.

Terrified.

Desperate.

Dying.

"Please..."

Roman froze.

Because the King — the devourer, the ancient one, the shadow-crowned god — had never said that word in his existence.

"Please... stop..."

Roman's voice was quiet.

"Why."

The King trembled.

"Because if you finish awakening...

I cease."

Roman stepped closer.

"And if I don't?"

The King swallowed — a human gesture that looked wrong on him.

"Then you become me."

Roman's breath hitched.

Langley's voice echoed faintly:

"Rome... choose carefully..."

The Rift pulsed.

The King knelt.

For the first time.

"Please."

CHAPTER 12 — Roman Rejects the Throne

The King knelt.

The Rift pulsed around him like a dying heart, shadows flickering violently as if the void itself were panicking.

Roman stood over him, the half-formed crown of shadow hovering above his head — not yet solid, not yet chosen, but waiting.

The King trembled.

"Please… do not finish awakening."

Roman stared at him.

At the monster who had hunted him.

At the shadow that had haunted his bloodline.

At the creature who had broken his father.

And for the first time…

Roman saw him clearly.

Not a god.

Not a king.

Not destiny.

A cycle.

A prison wearing a crown.

Roman's voice was quiet.

"I'm not becoming you."

The King's head snapped up, eyes wide with something Roman had never seen in him.

Terror.

"You cannot reject the throne."

Roman stepped back.

"I just did."

THE RIFT REACTS

The void convulsed.

Shadows recoiled.

The floor cracked.

The air screamed.

The half-crown above Roman's head flickered violently, destabilizing, glitching like a corrupted symbol.

The King staggered to his feet.

"STOP! YOU DO NOT UNDERSTAND WHAT YOU ARE DOING!"

Roman's voice deepened — not with power, but with conviction.

"I understand enough."

The King lunged.

Roman didn't move.

The shadows around him surged — not to protect him, not to attack, but to obey.

They grabbed the King mid-lunge, dragging him backward, pinning him to the shifting floor of the Rift.

The King screamed.

"YOU CANNOT BREAK THE CYCLE!"

Roman stepped closer.

"I'm not breaking it."

He leaned in.

"I'm ending it."

THE KING'S DESPERATION

The King thrashed against the shadows, his form glitching violently.

"If you reject the throne, the Rift collapses!"

Roman didn't blink. "Good."

"The world collapses with it!"

Roman's jaw tightened. "Then we rebuild."

"YOU DIE!"

Roman's eyes darkened.

"Then I die free."

The King froze.

Because no Sane had ever said that.

No heir had ever dared.

No vessel had ever refused.

Roman wasn't choosing power.

He wasn't choosing the throne.

He wasn't choosing the King.

He was choosing himself.

THE RIFT BEGINS TO TEAR

Cracks spread across the void — jagged lines of white light splitting the darkness. The Rift screamed, a sound like a thousand worlds dying at once.

Langley appeared at the edge of the void, her form flickering violently.

"ROME! STOP! YOU'RE COLLAPSING EVERYTHING!"

Roman turned to her.

His voice softened.

"I'm done being what he made me."

Langley reached for him — her hand passing through his arm like smoke.

"Rome… if you reject the throne, you won't survive this."

Roman looked at her — really looked at her.

At the sister he lost.

At the Herald she became.

At the shadow she was forced to wear.

"I'm not surviving," he said quietly.

"I'm choosing."

Langley's eyes filled with tears — black, shimmering, Rift-born tears.

"Rome… please…"

But Roman turned back to the King.

ROMAN'S FINAL WORD

The King screamed as the cracks widened, the Rift tearing itself apart.

"HEIR OF SANE — YOU CANNOT CHOOSE NOTHING!"

Roman stepped forward.

"I'm not choosing nothing."

He placed his hand on the King's chest.

The shadows recoiled.

The King convulsed.

Roman whispered:

"I'm choosing freedom."

The crown above his head shattered.

The Rift exploded.

And everything went white.

CHAPTER 13 — The Rift Explodes

White.

Not light.

Not purity.

Not salvation.

A violent, blinding white that burned through the darkness like a star dying in reverse.

Roman felt himself ripped backward — not falling, not flying, but being unmade. His body dissolved into shadow. His shadow dissolved into memory. His memory dissolved into something older.

The King screamed.

Not in rage.

Not in defiance.

In fear.

Because Roman had done the impossible.

He had said no.

And the Rift — the ancient engine that created kings, devoured heirs, and recycled bloodlines — didn't know how to process refusal.

It tore apart.

THE COLLAPSE

The void cracked like glass.

Shards of darkness fell upward.

Shards of light fell downward.

Time folded in on itself like a dying lung.

Roman's consciousness flickered.

He saw:

- His father kneeling
- His mother crying
- Langley dying
- Langley rising
- The King breaking
- The throne bleeding
- Himself crowned
- Himself dead
- Himself free

All at once.

The Rift screamed.

Roman screamed back.

THE KING'S LAST ATTEMPT

The King lunged through the collapsing void, his form glitching violently, half-shadow, half-man, half-memory.

"HEIR — STOP THIS!"

Roman didn't hear him.

Or maybe he did.

But he didn't care.

The King reached for him — not to kill him, not to claim him, but to anchor him.

"IF YOU FALL, YOU TAKE ME WITH YOU!"

Roman's voice was barely a whisper.

"Good."

The King's form convulsed.

"YOU DO NOT UNDERSTAND — WITHOUT A KING, THE RIFT HAS NO CENTER!"

Roman's eyes glowed.

"Then it collapses."

The King screamed — a sound of pure, ancient terror.

"AND THE WORLD COLLAPSES WITH IT!"

Roman's voice cracked.

"I'd rather end the world than become you."

The King froze.

Because no heir had ever said that.

Not once.

Not in a thousand cycles.

Not in a thousand kings.

Roman wasn't choosing death.

He was choosing freedom.

THE RIFT SHATTERS

The void ruptured.

A shockwave of white light tore through the collapsing darkness, ripping the King away from Roman, ripping Roman away from himself.

Langley's voice echoed faintly:

"ROME — HOLD ON — I'M COMING—"

But Roman couldn't hold on.

He was already gone.

OUTSIDE THE RIFT

James watched the sphere of darkness implode, collapsing inward like a dying star. Officers screamed. The street cracked. The sky dimmed.

Langley appeared beside him — fully formed, fully terrified.

James grabbed her. "Where is he. WHERE IS ROMAN."

Langley didn't answer.

Because she didn't know.

Because no one had ever rejected the throne.

Because no one had ever survived the collapse.

Because no one had ever fallen out of the Rift.

Her voice trembled.

"He's not dead."

James shook her. "Then where is he."

Langley looked at the empty space where the Rift had been.

Her voice was barely a whisper.

"He's somewhere the King can't reach."

James blinked. "Where is that."

Langley swallowed.

"Nowhere."

ROMAN AWAKENS

Roman gasped.

Air slammed into his lungs like a punch.

He opened his eyes.

He wasn't in the Rift.

He wasn't in the house.

He wasn't in the city.

He was lying on a cold, cracked surface under a sky that wasn't a sky — a swirling mass of white and black, light and shadow, creation and collapse.

A place between worlds.

A place outside the cycle.

A place no Sane had ever reached.

Roman whispered:

"…where am I."

A voice answered.

Not the King.

Not Langley.

Not human.

"You are where endings go."

Roman sat up slowly.

And saw a figure standing in the distance.

Tall.

Silent.

Watching.

Not the King.

Something older.

Something the King feared.

Something the throne served.

CHAPTER 14 — The Between: The Figure That Waits for Roman

Roman pushed himself up from the cracked, colorless ground. The air tasted like nothing — not cold, not warm, not breathable, not suffocating. Just absence.

The sky above him churned in slow spirals of white and black, like creation and collapse arguing with each other.

And the figure stood on the horizon.

Still.

Silent.

Watching.

Not approaching.

Not threatening.

Not hiding.

Waiting.

Roman swallowed hard. "Who are you."

The figure didn't answer.

It didn't need to.

Because Roman felt it.

A pressure behind his ribs.

A whisper in his blood.

Recognition is older than memory.

Langley's voice echoed faintly from nowhere and everywhere.

"Rome… don't go near it…"

Roman ignored her.

He stepped forward.

The ground rippled under his feet — not like water, not like shadow, but like reality adjusting to his presence.

The figure finally moved.

A single step.

And the Between trembled.

THE FIRST WORD

The figure's voice wasn't a sound.

It was a decision.

"No."

Roman froze.

"No what."

The figure tilted its head — not human, not inhuman, just… inevitable.

"No throne."

Roman's pulse quickened. "I rejected it."

The figure nodded once.

"Good."

Roman blinked. "Good?"

The figure took another step.

The Between shook again.

"The throne is a cage."

Roman's breath hitched.

The King had never said that.

Langley had never said that.

His father had never said that.

Roman whispered, "Then what are you."

The figure answered without hesitation.

"The one who built the cage."

Roman staggered backward.

"What— what does that mean."

The figure stepped closer.

It didn't grow larger.

The world grew smaller.

"I am the First Ending."

Roman's chest tightened.

"The first… King."

The figure shook its head.

"No."

It pointed toward the swirling sky.

"I am what the King fears."

Roman swallowed.

"And what do you want from me."

The figure's voice deepened — not louder, but heavier, like gravity choosing a direction.

"To see if you are different."

Roman's jaw clenched. "Different how."

The figure stepped close enough that Roman could finally see its face.

It was Roman's.

Older.

Hollow.

Crowned in nothing.

"Different from what I became."

Roman's breath stopped.

"You're me."

The figure nodded.

"I was."

THE TRUTH OF THE BETWEEN

The Between pulsed, revealing flashes of memory that weren't Roman's — but could have been.

A Roman who accepted the throne.

A Roman who devoured the King.

A Roman who ruled the Rift.

A Roman who became the next monster.

A Roman who was eventually replaced.

A Roman who ended up here.

The First Ending whispered:

"Every Sane who took the throne became me."

Roman shook his head violently.

"No. No, I'm not—"

The figure cut him off.

"You rejected the throne."

Roman steadied himself.

"Yes."

The figure stepped closer.

"Then you broke the cycle."

Roman's voice cracked.

"Is that good or bad."

The figure didn't blink.

"It is new."

Roman swallowed.

"And what happens now."

The First Ending leaned in, its voice a whisper that felt like a prophecy.

"Now you decide what replaces the throne."

Roman's stomach twisted.

"I don't want to replace anything."

The figure nodded.

"Then something else will."

Roman froze.

"What does that mean."

The First Ending stepped back, dissolving into the swirling sky.

Its final words echoed through the Between:

"If you do not choose a new order…

the world will choose one for you."

CHAPTER 15 — The City Falls

- ## James and the Officers vs. the Rapid Dead

The moment the Rift imploded, the city changed.

The air thickened.

The sky dimmed.

The shadows stretched like they were waking up.

James staggered backward, shielding his face from the shockwave. Officers around him scrambled for cover, some diving behind wrecked cars, others dragging the wounded away from the collapsing house.

Then the screaming started.

Not human screaming.

Fast. Wet. Wrong.

James spun toward the sound.

And saw them.

The rapid dead.

Not zombies — not anymore.

Not slow.

Not shambling.

Not mindless.

These things moved like animals that had been starved and then unleashed.

Bodies twisted.

Limbs bent at impossible angles.

Eyes glowing with the same shadow-sickness that had infected the city.

One officer whispered:

"Oh God… they're evolving."

James raised his weapon.

"No.

They're hungry."

THE FIRST WAVE

The rapid dead hit the officers like a tidal wave.

One leapt onto a cruiser, its spine cracking backward as it screamed. Another sprinted on all fours, faster than any human could track. A third slammed into an officer, tearing into him before he could even scream.

James fired three rounds into the closest one.

It didn't slow down.

He cursed under his breath. "Aim for the head!"

Officer Ramirez shouted back, "THEY DON'T HAVE HEADS ANYMORE!"

She wasn't wrong.

One of the creatures' skulls had split open like a flower, shadow-tendrils whipping outward as it charged.

James grabbed Ramirez and shoved her behind a wrecked SUV.

"Fall back! FALL BACK!"

But there was nowhere to fall back to.

The street was a warzone — overturned cars, burning buildings, bodies everywhere. The collapse of the Rift had triggered something in the infected.

They weren't just attacking.

They were hunting.

JAMES TAKES COMMAND

James slammed a fresh magazine into his rifle.

"Form a line! Keep them off the civilians!"

Officer Tran shouted, "There ARE no civilians!"

James didn't look at him.

"Then keep them off US!"

The officers formed a shaky firing line, raised weapons, breath trembling.

The rapid dead charged.

James fired.

Ramirez fired.

Tran fired.

Bullets tore through flesh, bone, shadow.

Some creatures fell.

Most didn't.

One sprinted across the hood of a car and launched itself at James. He ducked, grabbed it by the throat, and slammed it into the pavement. Its jaw snapped open, shadow spilling out like smoke.

James emptied half a magazine into its skull.

It finally stopped moving.

Ramirez shouted, "Captain! They're flanking!"

James spun.

She was right.

The rapid dead were learning.

They were circling.

Coordinating.

Communicating.

James whispered:

"…Roman… where the hell are you…"

THE SECOND WAVE

A shriek tore through the street — louder, deeper, angrier.

The rapid dead froze.

Then they moved.

All at once.

James barely had time to shout:

"BRACE!"

The creatures hit the line like a hurricane.

Tran went down first, dragged screaming into a pile of bodies. Ramirez fired point-blank into a creature's chest, but it didn't stop until James tackled it off her.

Another officer was lifted into the air by a creature with elongated limbs, its fingers digging into his ribs.

James fired upward, dropping both.

He didn't have time to check if the officer survived.

He already knew the answer.

THE TURNING POINT

A creature lunged at James from behind.

He spun too slowly.

He knew he was dead.

But a blast of light — white, sharp, unnatural — tore through the creature's torso, vaporizing it.

James blinked.

Ramirez stared.

Tran — bleeding, barely conscious — whispered:

"…what was that…"

James looked up.

The sky flickered.

Not lightning.

Not fire.

Not shadow.

Something else.

Something Roman-shaped.

Something Roman-sized.

Something Roman-born.

James whispered:

"…Roman…?"

But the sky didn't answer.

The rapid dead did.

They screamed — all at once — and charged again.

James raised his weapon.

"Hold the line!"

CHAPTER 16 — The Rapid Dead Mutate

The second wave hit the officers like a storm of teeth and shadow.

James fired until his rifle clicked empty, then slammed a fresh magazine in with shaking hands. Ramirez dragged Tran behind a wrecked cruiser, blood soaking through her sleeves.

The rapid dead screamed — a sound like metal tearing — and then something changed.

They stopped.

All at once.

Every creature froze mid-charge, mid-crawl, mid-lunge. Their bodies twitched violently, spasming like puppets with cut strings.

James whispered:

"…what the hell…"

Ramirez raised her weapon. "Captain… something's wrong with them."

Wrong didn't cover it.

The creatures' spines arched backward. Their jaws unhinged. Their limbs stretched, bones cracking, reshaping. Shadow poured from their mouths like smoke being sucked inward.

James felt the air shift — heavy, electric, wrong.

Tran whispered:

"…they're mutating…"

THE FIRST MUTATION

One of the rapid dead — a woman in a shredded hospital gown — convulsed violently. Her skin split along her arms, peeling back like wet paper. Something underneath pushed outward.

Not bone.

Not muscle.

Not shadow.

Something **new**.

Her fingers elongated into hooked talons. Her jaw split into three segments. Her eyes — once glowing with shadow — now burned with a pale, unnatural white.

James fired.

The bullet hit her square in the forehead.

She didn't fall.

She didn't even flinch.

She turned her head toward him, her neck cracking like a branch.

Ramirez whispered:

"...Captain... they're adapting to gunfire..."

James raised his weapon anyway.

"Then we shoot harder."

THE SECOND MUTATION

Another creature — this one missing half its torso — began to grow something from its spine. A long, whip-like appendage of bone and shadow, snapping through the air like a living blade.

It lashed out.

An officer screamed as the appendage sliced through his vest, carving a deep gash across his chest.

James grabbed him, dragging him behind cover.

"Ramirez! Tran! FALL BACK!"

But the creatures weren't giving them space.

They were evolving.

Fast.

One creature's legs fused together, forming a single, powerful limb that launched it forward like a spear. Another's ribcage split open, revealing a cluster of tendrils that writhed like searching hands.

Ramirez fired a shotgun blast into one of the tendrils.

It grabbed the shotgun.

And crushed it.

James stared.

"…they're learning…"

THE THIRD MUTATION- THE HIVE CALL

A deep, resonant hum vibrated through the street.

Every mutated creature stopped.

Their heads snapped upward.

Their bodies stiffened.

And then they screamed — not in pain, not in hunger, but in **response**.

James felt the hair on his arms rise.

"What the hell was that."

Tran coughed blood. "A signal… Captain… they're being called…"

Ramirez shook her head. "By whom?"

James didn't answer.

Because he already knew.

Not the King.
Not the Rift.
Not Roman.

Something else.

Something that woke up when Roman rejected the throne.

Something that filled the vacuum.

Something that the world wanted.

THE MUTATED HORDE CHARGES

The creatures' bodies finished reshaping — faster, stronger, smarter, coordinated.

James raised his weapon.

"Hold the line!"

The mutated rapid dead charged.

Not like zombies.

Like soldiers.

Like predators.

Like a new species.

Ramirez screamed, "CAPTAIN—"

James fired.

Tran fired.

Ramirez fired.

The street lit up with muzzle flashes.

The creatures didn't slow.

They didn't hesitate.

They didn't fear it.

They **evolved**.

CHAPTER 17 — The Mutated Horde Overwhelms the Line

The mutated rapid dead charged as one a coordinated, unnatural stampede of bone, shadow, and hunger.

James fired until his rifle overheated, smoke rising from the barrel. Ramirez emptied her last shotgun shells. Tran, bleeding out, still managed to squeeze off a few rounds.

None of it mattered.

The creatures didn't slow.

They **accelerated**.

One vaulted over a burning sedan, landing on all fours like a spider made of broken limbs. Another sprinted along a wall, claws digging into brick as it launched itself toward the officers. A third slithered across the pavement, its ribcage opening like a mouth.

James shouted:

"FALL BACK! FALL—"

A creature slammed into him mid-command, knocking him into the side of a cruiser. His vision blurred. He felt claws rake across his vest, tearing fabric, scraping ribs.

Ramirez tackled the creature off him, stabbing it with a broken piece of rebar. It shrieked — not in pain, but in **rage** — and threw her across the street like a rag doll.

James staggered to his feet.

"RAMIREZ!"

She didn't move.

THE LINE BREAKS

The officers' formation collapsed.

One creature grabbed an officer by the leg and dragged him screaming into a pile of bodies. Another leapt onto the hood of a cruiser and smashed through the windshield, pulling the driver out in a spray of glass.

Tran tried to crawl away, leaving a trail of blood behind him.

A mutated rapid dead — its jaw split into three segments — crawled toward him, clicking its teeth like a predator savoring the moment.

James fired.

The bullet hit the creature's skull.

It didn't stop.

It didn't even blink.

James whispered:

"…they're unstoppable…"

THE HORDE EVOLVES MID-BATTLE

The creatures convulsed again — mid-charge, mid-kill, mid-scream.

Their bodies twisted.

Bones rearranged.

Limbs elongated.

Eyes multiplied.

One creature sprouted a second pair of arms.

Another grew a tail of segmented bone.

A third's spine extended outward, forming a jagged ridge of blades.

James felt his stomach drop.

They weren't just mutating.

They were **adapting to the fight**.

Ramirez groaned, pushing herself up on shaking arms.

"Captain… they're evolving every time we hit them…"

James grabbed her, pulling her behind cover.

"They're not evolving."

He looked at the horde — at the way they moved, coordinated, communicated.

"They're being **guided**."

Ramirez swallowed.

"By whom."

James didn't answer.

Because he already knew.

Something woke up when Roman rejected the throne.
Something filled the vacuum.
Something wanted the world.

THE OFFICERS ARE OVERRUN

A creature slammed into the cruiser James and Ramirez hid behind, flipping it onto its side. The impact threw them both into the street.

James rolled, coughing blood.

Ramirez screamed as a creature pinned her down, its talons digging into the asphalt beside her head.

James fired.

The bullet ricocheted off the creature's skull.

It turned toward him.

Its eyes — all six of them — burned with pale white light.

It lunged.

James braced for death.

But another creature slammed into him from the side, knocking him into a pile of debris. He hit the ground hard, ribs cracking.

He couldn't breathe.

He couldn't move.

He could only watch as the mutated horde swarmed the last surviving officers, dragging them into the shadows, tearing through armor, ripping through steel.

The street became a feeding ground.

James whispered:

"...Roman... please... come back..."

FINAL MOMENT BEFORE COLLAPSE

A massive creature — taller than a man, its spine arched like a scorpion's tail — crawled toward James. Its breath was hot, wet, and rancid. Its claws scraped the pavement.

James raised his empty weapon.

He knew it wouldn't matter.

The creature reared back.

Ready to strike.

Ready to kill.

Ready to end him.

And then—

The sky cracked.

A beam of white light — sharp, unnatural, familiar — tore through the clouds and slammed into the street between James and the creature.

The shockwave vaporized three mutated rapid dead instantly.

James shielded his face.

Ramirez screamed.

Tran whispered:

"…that's Roman… it has to be…"

The creature hissed and backed away, its body trembling.

The hordes froze.

The light pulsated again.

And the city held its breath.

CHAPTER 18 — The Mutated Horde destroys the Line

The beam of white light faded.

Silence followed.

Not peace. Not safety.

The kind of silence predators make when they're deciding who to kill first.

James pushed himself up, ribs screaming, vision swimming. Ramirez crawled toward him, blood dripping from her forehead. Tran lay motionless, barely breathing.

The mutated rapid dead stared at the fading light in the sky — trembling, twitching, reacting like animals hearing a sound only they understood.

Then they turned.

All of them.

Toward the officers.

James whispered:

"…oh God…"

And the hordes of mutated zombies charged.

THE COLLAPSE OF THE LAST DEFENSE

The first creature hit James like a truck, knocking him backward into a pile of debris. He rolled, barely avoiding a talon that sliced through the concrete where his head had been.

Ramirez fired her sidearm — three shots, clean hits.

The creature didn't slow.

It grabbed her by the throat and slammed her into the hood of a car. The metal caved inward. Ramirez gasped, clawing at its hand.

James lunged, tackling the creature off her. It shrieked, twisting mid-fall, landing on all fours like a spider.

More creatures swarmed.

One grabbed Tran's leg and dragged him screaming into the shadows. His voice cut off abruptly.

James fired wildly, trying to cover Ramirez.

"GET UP! MOVE!"

She tried.

She couldn't.

A creature with a split jaw and too many eyes crawled over the car toward her, saliva dripping in thick black strings.

James sprinted.

He wasn't fast enough.

THE HORDE EVOLVES AGAIN

The creatures convulsed mid-charge — bones cracking, limbs elongating, eyes multiplying. Their bodies reshaped themselves in real time, adapting to the officers' movements.

One grew a second pair of arms. Another sprouted bone spines along its back. A third's legs fused into a single, powerful limb that launched it forward like a spear.

James fired point-blank into one's chest.

It absorbed the impact.

Its ribs opened like a mouth.

James stumbled back.

"…they're evolving every second…"

Ramirez screamed as a creature pinned her down, its talons digging into the asphalt beside her head.

James raised his weapon.

Empty.

He threw it.

The creature barely noticed.

The Overrun

The horde swarmed.

One creature slammed James into a wall, cracking the brick behind him. Another grabbed his arm and twisted until his shoulder popped. A third clawed at his vest, tearing through fabric and skin.

James roared in pain, kicking, punching, fighting with everything he had left.

It wasn't enough.

Ramirez's scream cut through the chaos.

"CAPTAIN!"

James turned.

A creature had her pinned, its jaw splitting open, shadow pouring out like smoke.

James tried to run.

Another creature tackled him, slamming him into the pavement.

He tasted blood.

He tasted dirt.

He tasted the end.

The mutated hordes closed in.

Dozens of them.

Hundreds.

A tidal wave of teeth and shadow.

James whispered:

"...Roman... please..."

A creature raised its talons.

Ready to kill.

Ready to end him.

THE MOMENT BEFORE DEATH

The hordes froze.

Every creature stopped mid-strike.

Their bodies twitched violently, like puppets whose strings had been yanked.

Their eyes — all of them — turned upward.

Toward the sky.

Toward the crack forming in the clouds.

Toward the light that wasn't lightning.

Toward something **returning**.

James blinked through blood and dust.

"...Roman...?"

The creatures hissed.

Not in fear.

In **recognition**.

The sky split open.

White light poured through.

And the horde screamed.

CHAPTER 19 — Langley Appears to James

The mutated creature loomed over James, its talons raised, its jaw splitting open like a blooming wound. James braced himself, breath ragged, ribs screaming, vision tunneling.

He whispered:

"…Roman… I'm sorry…"

The creature struck—

—and froze.

Mid-air. Mid-kill. Mid-scream.

Held in place by **nothing**.

No force. No hand. No visible restraint

Just **stopped**.

James blinked through blood and dust.

"What… the hell…"

The creature twitched, trying to move, but its limbs were locked in place like time itself had grabbed it by the throat.

A voice behind James whispered:

"Don't move."

James spun.

And saw her.

Langley.

Not the girl from Roman's memories. Not the Herald from the Rift. Not the sister he'd only heard about in whispers.

A woman made of shadow and light, flickering like a dying bulb, her eyes glowing with a soft, unnatural silver.

She stepped forward, her feet not quite touching the ground.

James stared, breath caught in his throat.

"…Langley… Sane…"

She tilted her head, studying him.

"You're James."

James swallowed hard.

"You're supposed to be dead."

Langley's expression didn't change.

"I am."

THE HORDE REACTS

The mutated rapid dead shrieked — all of them — a sound of pure, primal terror. They backed away from Langley, their bodies convulsing, their mutations glitching like corrupted files.

One creature's extra limb retracted. Another's bone spines crumbled. A third collapsed entirely, its body unable to hold shape in her presence.

James whispered:

"…they're afraid of you…"

Langley didn't look at him.

"They should be."

She raised her hand.

The creature frozen above James shattered — not into blood, not into bone, but into **shadow dust**, dissolving into the air like smoke.

James scrambled backward.

"Jesus Christ—"

Langley turned to him sharply.

"Don't say His name here."

James froze.

"…why."

Langley looked at the sky — at the crack widening, at the white light bleeding through.

"Because He's not the one listening."

Langley Saves James

She knelt beside him, her form flickering.

James flinched.

She frowned.

"If I wanted you dead, you'd be dust."

James forced himself to breathe.

"…Roman… is he alive?"

Langley's expression softened — barely.

"Yes."

James exhaled shakily.

"Where is he?"

Langley looked at the sky again.

"Somewhere the King can't reach."

James frowned.

"What does that mean?"

Langley stood.

The mutated horde shrieked again — louder, angrier, more desperate. They circled the two of them, but none dared cross the invisible boundary around her.

Langley extended her hand toward James.

"It means you need to get up."

James hesitated.

"Why."

Langley's eyes darkened.

"Because something else is coming."

James swallowed.

"…worse than them?"

Langley nodded once.

"Much."

The Warning

James took her hand.

Her touch was cold. Not dead cold. Not supernatural cold.

Between-worlds cold.

Langley pulled him to his feet with ease that didn't match her size.

James steadied himself.

"What do we do?"

Langley looked at the sky — at the crack widening, at the light pulsing, at the world bending.

Her voice dropped to a whisper.

"We survive long enough for Roman to come back."

James stared at her.

"And if he doesn't?"

Langley didn't blink.

"Then the world ends."

CHAPTER 20 — Langley Unleashed: The Herald vs. the Horde

The mutated rapid dead circled James and Langley, their bodies twitching, their new limbs scraping the pavement. They hissed, clicked, shrieked — a chorus of hunger and evolution.

Langley stepped forward.

Alone.

Her shadow stretched behind her like a living thing, splitting into tendrils that curled and uncurled like fingers eager for violence.

James whispered:

"...Langley... don't—"

She didn't look back.

"Stay behind me."

The horde charged.

And Langley moved.

SHADOWFORM — THE FIRST CUT

The first creature leapt at her, claws extended.

Langley dissolved.

Her body turned into a smear of black smoke, the creature passing through her harmlessly. She reformed behind it, one hand raised.

She whispered:

"Down."

The creature's spine snapped in three places at once — without her touching it. It collapsed into a heap of twitching limbs.

The horde hesitated.

James stared.

"Holy—"

Langley vanished again.

VEIL SIGHT — THE SECOND STRIKE

She reappeared above the horde, suspended in the air like gravity forgot her.

Her eyes glowed silver.

She saw everything — every mutation, every weak point, every unstable bone, every shadow-sickness knot inside their bodies.

She raised her hand.

"Break."

Twenty creatures convulsed simultaneously, their mutations unraveling, their bodies collapsing inward like crushed cans.

The street shook.

The horde screamed.

James whispered:

"...she's reading their biology..."

Langley whispered back — though she was thirty feet away:

"I'm reading their fate."

MIND-TOUCH — THE THIRD STRIKE

A massive creature — the size of a truck, its spine arched like a scorpion's tail — lunged at her.

Langley didn't dodge.

She touched its forehead with one finger.

Its entire body froze.

Its eyes widened.

It saw something — something only Langley could show it.

A memory.
A truth.
A death.

The creature screamed until its throat tore open.

Then it fell.

James staggered.

"What did you do to it?"

Langley floated down, her feet barely touching the ground.

"I reminded it what it used to be."

HERALD'S CALL — THE FOURTH STRIKE

The horde regrouped.

Hundreds of them.

Mutated.

Evolved.

Coordinated.

They charged as one.

Langley inhaled.

The air bent around her.

She exhaled.

The Herald's Call tore through the street — a shockwave of pure, ancient resonance. Windows shattered. Cars flipped. The pavement cracked.

The horde flew backward in a wave of bodies, slamming into buildings, walls, each other.

Some disintegrated.

Some melted into shadow.

Some simply ceased.

James shielded his face, barely staying on his feet.

"LANGLEY! YOU'LL LEVEL THE BLOCK!"

Langley didn't answer.

She wasn't done.

SHADOWFORM: ASCENSION — THE FINAL STRIKE

The remaining creatures — the strongest, the most mutated — crawled toward her, trembling but unwilling to flee.

Langley rose into the air.

Her shadow rose with her.

It expanded.

Stretched.

Split into dozens of tendrils.

Then hundreds.

Then thousands.

A storm of living darkness.

James whispered:

"…Roman wasn't the only one chosen…"

Langley's voice echoed from everywhere and nowhere:

"I am the Herald."

The shadow-storm descended.

It tore through the horde like a hurricane of knives and smoke.

Creatures were shredded.

Crushed.

Pulled apart.

Erased.

In seconds, the street was empty.

Silent.

Dead.

Langley landed gently, her shadow returning to normal, her eyes dimming.

She turned to James.

"We need to move."

James stared at the carnage.

"…you did all that alone…"

Langley nodded.

"And that was restraint."

James swallowed.

"...what happens when you don't restrain yourself?"

Langley looked at the sky — at the crack widening, at the light pulsing.

Her voice dropped to a whisper.

"Pray we never find out."

CHAPTER 21 — Flight Through the Ruins

- **James & Langley Escape the Dead City**

The street was silent.

Not peaceful.
Not safe.
The kind of silence that follows a massacre.

Langley stood in the center of the devastation she created — shadows still curling around her ankles like smoke that hadn't decided whether to dissipate or kill again.

James staggered to his feet, clutching his ribs.

He looked at her.

At the bodies.
At the dust.
At the absence of anything still moving.

"…you did all this…"

Langley didn't answer.

She didn't need to.

Her eyes were fixed on the sky — on the widening crack, on the white light pulsing through it like a heartbeat.

James limped toward her.

"We need to get out of here."

Langley finally turned.

"Yes. Before the next wave."

James froze.

"...next wave?"

Langley didn't blink.

"The horde wasn't the threat. They were the warning."

THE CITY BEGINS TO SHIFT

As they moved through the street, the ground trembled beneath their feet. Buildings groaned. Windows cracked. Streetlights flickered.

James looked around.

"What's happening now?"

Langley didn't slow.

"The city is reacting to the collapse."

James frowned.

"Reacting how?"

Langley pointed.

A building two blocks away folded inward like it was made of paper, collapsing into itself without a sound.

James whispered:

"…Jesus…"

Langley shot him a sharp look.

"I told you. Don't say His name here."

James swallowed.

"Right. Sorry."

THE PATH THROUGH THE RUINS

They moved fast — or rather, Langley moved fast and James tried not to die keeping up.

Every street they crossed was worse than the last:

- Cars fused into the asphalt
- Shadows moving without light
- Bodies half-absorbed into walls
- Air that tasted like metal and ash

James coughed.

"This place is… wrong."

Langley nodded.

"It's becoming Between."

James stopped.

"Between? Like where Roman is?"

Langley didn't turn around.

"Yes. The collapse is bleeding into the world."

James felt his stomach drop.

"So, the city is… merging with that place?"

Langley finally looked at him.

"If Roman doesn't return soon, the world will."

James didn't ask what that meant.

He didn't want to know.

THE SHADOWS START FOLLOW

As they reached an intersection, Langley suddenly raised her hand.

James froze.

"What? What is it?"

Langley's eyes narrowed.

"We're being followed."

James spun, raised the weapon.

He saw nothing.

"By what?"

Langley whispered:

"Not what. Who."

James felt a chill crawl up his spine.

"Who?"

Langley stepped closer to him, her voice low.

"Something that woke up when Roman rejected the throne."

James tightened his grip on his weapon.

"And what does it want?"

Langley didn't answer.

She didn't need to.

A shadow moved across the rooftop above them — tall, thin, wrong.

James aimed.

"LANGLEY—"

Langley grabbed his arm.

"Don't shoot. You'll only make it hungry."

James stared at her.

"...hungry?"

Langley nodded once.

"For you."

THE ESCAPE

She grabbed his wrist.

"Move."

They ran.

Through alleys that bent the wrong direction.

Past buildings that whispered.

Under streetlights that flickered like dying stars.

James gasped for breath, pain stabbing through his ribs.

"Where are we going?"

Langley didn't look back.

"Somewhere it can't follow."

James stumbled.

"And where is that?"

Langley's voice was barely a whisper.

"Anywhere Roman still exists."

James blinked.

"...what does that mean—"

A roar shook the street behind them.

Not the horde.

Not the King.

Not anything James had heard before.

Langley tightened her grip.

"Run."

And they did.

CHAPTER 22 — The Siblings Ascend

- ### The Death That Changes Everything

The moment their mother died, the world didn't just shake.

It **screamed**.

Langley felt it first — a tearing sensation in her chest, like someone had ripped out the last piece of her humanity. She staggered, clutching her ribs, eyes widening as the truth hit her like a blade.

James saw her collapse.

"Langley—?"

She didn't answer.

She **howled**.

A sound that wasn't human.
A sound that wasn't Herald.
A sound that made the mutated horde freeze mid-step.

Then Roman felt it.

In the Between.

The moment the truth reached him, the white sky cracked. The ground split. The First Ending recoiled as Roman's aura ignited — not shadow, not darkness, not Rift-born power.

Something **holy**.

Something the Between had never seen.

Roman whispered:

"…Mom…"

And the Between **exploded**.

LANGLEY'S DESCENT — THE DARK HERALD

Langley rose slowly from the ground, her body flickering like a dying star. But she wasn't dying.

She was **transforming**.

Her shadow stretched across the street, splitting into tendrils that were writhed like serpents. Her eyes turned pitch-black, swallowing the whites entirely. Her voice layered itself — human, Herald, and something deeper.

James backed away.

"Langley… what's happening to you…"

She didn't look at him.

She looked at the horde.

And the horde **backed away**.

Langley whispered:

"You killed her."

The shadows around her surged.

"You killed our mother."

The mutated rapid dead shrieked, scrambling over each other to escape.

Too late.

Langley vanished.

And the slaughter began.

SHADOW ASCENSION — LANGLEY UNBOUND

She reappeared in the center of the horde, her body dissolving into a vortex of black smoke. Tendrils shot outward, impaling creatures through skulls, spines, hearts.

One creature tried to flee.

Langley appeared in front of it.

She grabbed its jaw.

And **ripped**.

Shadow and bone sprayed across the pavement.

Another creature leapt at her.

She caught it mid-air with a single hand.

Her voice was a whisper of pure hatred.

"You took her from us."

She crushed its skull like wet clay.

The horde panicked.

They ran.

They screamed.

They mutated in desperation.

Langley didn't care.

She hunted.

She tore.

She devoured.

Every kill pulled her deeper into the dark.
Every scream fed the Herald.
Every death made her less Langley…
and more **what the King feared**.

James watched it in horror.

"Langley— STOP! You're losing yourself!"

She turned toward him.

Her eyes were bottomless.

"I don't care."

ROMAN'S ASCENT — THE DIVINE RETURN

The Between shattered.

Roman fell through the crack in the sky like a meteor of white fire. His body glowed with a brilliance that wasn't shadow, wasn't Rift, wasn't King.

It was **creation**.

He hit the ground with a shockwave that vaporized a dozen mutated creatures instantly.

James shielded his face.

"ROMAN!"

Roman stood slowly.

His eyes glowed white.
His veins pulsed with light.
His shadow was gone — replaced by a halo of shimmering energy.

He wasn't the King.
He wasn't the Heir.
He wasn't the Replacement.

He was something **new**.

Something the throne had never accounted for.

Something the First Ending had feared.

Roman looked at the horde.

He didn't shout.

He didn't roar.

He didn't threaten.

He simply said:

"You killed my mother."

The world trembled.

DIVINE SURGE — ROMAN UNLEASHED

The horde charged.

Roman raised his hand.

A wave of white fire erupted outward, incinerating everything in a 50-foot radius. Creatures melted into ash mid-scream. Buildings shook. The pavement cracked.

One creature — massive, mutated beyond recognition — lunged at him.

Roman stepped forward.

His hand pierced its chest like it was made of smoke.

He whispered:

"You don't get to exist anymore."

The creature disintegrated.

Another tried to flank him.

Roman turned his head slightly.

A beam of light shot from his eyes, slicing the creature in half.

James stared.

"…Roman… what are you…"

Roman didn't answer.

He walked through the battlefield like a storm given human shape, every step unleashing another blast of divine power.

He wasn't fighting.

He was **avenging**.

THE SIBLINGS — DARK AND DIVINE

Langley landed beside him, covered in shadow and blood, her eyes black voids.

Roman stood tall, glowing like a fallen star.

The horde — what remained of it — trembled.

For the first time in their existence…

They understood fear.

Roman looked at Langley.

"Lang… we're not done."

Langley's voice was a whisper of darkness.

"No. We're just getting started."

The siblings turned toward the remaining horde.

One divine.

One damned.

Both unstoppable.

And together?

They were extinction.

CHAPTER 23 — THE SIBLINGS UNLEASHED - *ROMAN & LANGLEY FIGHT SIDE BY SIDE*

The battlefield was a graveyard of ash and shadow.

The sky cracked with white fire.

The ground pulsed with darkness.

And in the center of it all stood the Sane siblings.

Roman — glowing with divine radiance, eyes burning white, every breath shaking the air.

Langley — wrapped in living shadow, eyes black voids, her aura bending reality around her.

The mutated horde hesitated.

Not because they recognized them.

Because they **felt** them.

Two forces that should never exist at the same time.

Two halves of a broken destiny.

Two children mourning the same mother.

Roman stepped forward.

Langley stepped with him.

James whispered:

"…oh my God…"

Langley didn't look back.

"He's not the one you should be praying to."

THE FIRST WAVE — LIGHT & SHADOW

The horde charged.

Roman raised his hand.

A beam of white fire erupted from his palm, slicing through the first line of creatures like they were made of smoke. Bodies disintegrated mid-scream, ash swirling into the air.

Langley vanished.

She reappeared behind the second line, her shadow tendrils impaling three creatures at once. She twisted her wrist — the tendrils snapped their spines like twigs.

Roman slammed his fist into the ground.

A shockwave of divine energy rippled outward, vaporizing a dozen more.

Langley leapt into the air, dissolving into a storm of black smoke that shredded everything it touched.

They moved like they'd trained together for centuries.

They hadn't.

They were simply born for this.

THE SECOND WAVE — THE SIBLING SYNC

A massive creature — mutated beyond recognition, its spine arched like a scorpion's tail — lunged at Roman.

Langley appeared on its back.

She whispered:

"Fall."

The creature collapsed, its limbs folding inward as if crushed by invisible hands.

Roman stepped over its corpse.

"Thanks."

Langley smirked — a dark, dangerous curl of her lips.

"Don't get used to it."

Another wave charged.

Roman raised his hand.

Langley raised hers.

Light and shadow spiraled together — not fighting, not clashing, but **syncing**.

A beam of white fire wrapped in black tendrils erupted outward, tearing through the horde in a perfect arc.

Creatures exploded into dust.

Buildings shook.

The sky cracked wider.

James shielded his face.

"…they're unstoppable…"

THE THIRD WAVE — THE SANE BLOODLINE AWAKENS

The horde mutated again desperately, terrified, evolving in real time.

Extra limbs.

Bone armor.

Shadow-spines.

New jaws.

New eyes.

Roman didn't flinch.

Langley didn't blink.

They stepped forward together.

Roman unleashed a blast of divine energy that lit the entire block. Langley unleashed a vortex of shadow that swallowed the survivors.

One creature — massive, armored, roaring — broke through the blast and charged Roman.

Langley moved first.

She grabbed its throat.

Her voice was a whisper of pure hatred.

"You killed our mother."

Roman placed his hand on its chest.

His voice was a whisper of pure grief.

"Goodbye."

The creature disintegrated between them.

THE FINAL WAVE — DIVINE & DAMNED

The last of the horde gathered — hundreds of them — forming a wall of mutated flesh and shadow.

Roman's aura flared.

Langley's shadow expanded.

They looked at each other.

Roman nodded.

Langley nodded back.

And they charged.

Roman moved like a storm — every strike a blast of white fire, every step a shockwave, every breath a command to the world to obey.

Langley moved like a nightmare — teleporting, dissolving, impaling, ripping, her shadow doing the killing before her hands even reached the target.

They tore through the horde like gods.

Not because they wanted power.

Because they wanted **justice**.

Because they wanted **vengeance**.

Because someone killed their mother.

And the world needed to understand what that meant.

AFTERMATH — THE SIBLINGS STAND ALONE

When the last creature fell, the city was silent.

Roman stood in the center of the ruins, glowing like a fallen star.

Langley stood beside him, shadows curling around her like a cloak.

James approached slowly.

"...Roman... Langley... what are you two now..."

Roman looked at his hands — still glowing.

Langley looked at her shadow — still hungry.

They answered at the same time.

Roman: **"Something new."**

Langley: **"Something terrible."**

They looked at each other.

And for the first time…

They were afraid.

Not of the horde.

Not of the King.

Not of the world.

Of what they were becoming.

CHAPTER 24 — Langley's Sacrifice

The battlefield was quiet.

Too quiet.

Roman's divine aura dimmed as he turned toward Langley. She stood perfectly still; her shadow stretched across the ruins like a living stain. Her chest rose and fell too fast. Her fingers twitched. Her eyes — once black voids — now swirled with something deeper.

Something bottomless.

James whispered:

"…Roman… something's wrong with her…"

Roman stepped towards her.

"Langley."

She didn't answer.

Her shadow did.

It rose behind her like a second body — taller, sharper, monstrous.

Roman's voice softened.

"Lang… look at me."

She did.

And Roman's heart dropped.

Because her eyes weren't just dark.

They were **empty**.

THE DARKNESS TAKES HER

Langley's body convulsed.

Her shadow exploded outward, tendrils whipping through the air like blades. The ground cracked beneath her feet. The air bent around her like gravity was trying to escape.

James stumbled back.

"Roman—!"

Roman raised a hand.

"Stay behind me."

Langley screamed.

Not in pain.
Not in rage.
In **transformation**.

Her voice layered itself — human, Herald, and something ancient.

"I can't hold it—"

Her shadow surged.

"I CAN'T HOLD IT—"

Roman reached for her.

"Langley, listen to me—"

She vanished.

SHADOW ASCENSION — UNBOUND

She reappeared above the ruins, suspended in the air, her body dissolving into a vortex of black smoke. Her hair whipped around her like tendrils. Her arms stretched unnaturally. Her shadow expanded until it covered the entire block.

The mutated horde — what remained of it — screamed and fled.

Langley didn't let them.

Her voice echoed across the city:

"YOU TOOK HER FROM US."

A shockwave of shadow erupted outward.

Creatures were ripped apart mid-run.
Buildings cracked.
Streetlights shattered.
The sky dimmed.

Roman shielded James with a wall of divine light.

"LANGLEY! STOP!"

She didn't hear him.

Or she didn't care.

THE SLAUGHTER BEGINS

Langley descended like a falling star of darkness.

She hit the ground with a blast of shadow that vaporized everything within fifty feet. Tendrils shot outward, impaling creatures, dragging them screaming into the dark.

One creature tried to crawl away.

Langley appeared in front of it.

She grabbed its skull.

Her voice was a whisper of pure hatred.

"You killed our mother."

She crushed its head like wet clay.

Roman flinched.

"Langley… please…"

She turned toward him.

Her face was twisted — not monstrous, not demonic, but **broken**.

"I can't stop it."

Her shadow surged again.

"I DON'T WANT TO STOP IT."

ROMAN REALIZES THE TRUTH

Roman stepped forward, divine aura flaring.

"Langley, listen to me—"

She screamed.

Her shadow lashed out, striking Roman with enough force to crack the pavement beneath him. He slid backward, boots carving trenches in the ground.

James stared in horror.

"She's attacking YOU!"

Roman wiped blood from his lip.

"No.
She's attacking everything."

Langley floated above them, her shadow forming a monstrous silhouette behind her — wings, claws, teeth, shapes that didn't belong to any world.

Her voice shook the air.

"I AM THE HERALD."

The shadow behind her roared.

"AND THE HERALD SERVES NO ONE."

Roman's eyes widened.

"…she's losing herself…"

James whispered:

"She's becoming the King."

Roman shook his head.

"No."

His aura flared brighter.

"She's becoming something worse."

THE DARK HERALD AWAKENS

Langley's shadow expanded until it swallowed the entire street. The world dimmed. The air freezes. The ground cracked.

She raised her hand.

Every remaining creature — even the ones trying to hide — was dragged screaming into the air by invisible force.

Langley clenched her fist.

They imploded.

Roman shouted:

"LANGLEY, STOP!"

She turned toward him slowly.

Her voice was a whisper of death.

"Why?"

Roman stepped forward.

"Because you're not a monster."

Langley's expression twisted.

Her shadow surged.

"I AM NOW."

CHAPTER 25 — The Essence Transfer

Langley hovered above the ruins, her shadow stretching across the city like a living eclipse. Her body flickered between human and something monstrous. Her eyes were bottomless voids. Her voice was layered with too many tones.

Roman stepped forward, divine aura blazing.

"Langley… fight it."

She didn't hear him.

Or she couldn't.

Her shadow surged outward, swallowing the street, the buildings, the sky. The world dimmed around her. The air freezes. The ground cracked.

James whispered:

"…Roman… something's coming…"

Roman felt it too.

A pressure.
A presence.
A hunger older than the King.

The shadows behind Langley twisted.

And something stepped out.

THE ENTITY — THE VOID THAT WATCHES

It didn't walk.

It didn't float.

It didn't exist in a way the human mind could understand.

It simply **appeared**.

A tall, thin silhouette made of absence — not shadow, not darkness, but the *space where light dies*. Its edges flickered like a glitch in reality. Its face was a smooth void, featureless, expressionless, endless.

James fell to his knees.

"What… what is that…"

Roman's voice dropped to a whisper.

"…the thing the throne was built to contain…"

The Entity tilted its head toward Langley.

And she froze.

Her shadow stopped moving.

Her body stopped flickering.

Her scream died in her throat.

The Entity spoke without sound.

"Herald."

Langley's eyes widened — not in fear, but in recognition.

"No…"

Roman stepped forward.

"Get away from her."

The Entity ignored him.

It reached out a hand — long, thin, impossible — and touched Langley's forehead.

Her body convulsed violently.

Her shadow exploded outward.

Roman shouted:

"LANGLEY!"

THE CLAIMING BEGINS

Langley's scream tore through the city — a sound of pure agony and pure surrender. Her shadow wrapped around her like chains. Her body twisted, contorted, reshaped.

The Entity whispered:

"You were born for this."

Langley shook her head violently.

"No— NO— I'm not—"

The Entity's hand tightened.

"You are mine."

Roman's aura flared white-hot.

"LET HER GO!"

He launched a beam of divine fire at the Entity.

It passed through the Entity like light through smoke.

The Entity didn't even turn.

Roman staggered.

"…that's impossible…"

James shouted:

"ROMAN! DO SOMETHING!"

Roman tried.

He unleashed everything — divine blasts, shockwaves, radiant strikes — but nothing touched the Entity. Every attack passed through it like it wasn't there.

Because it wasn't.

Not fully.

Not yet.

LANGLEY'S TRANSFORMATION

Langley's body lifted into the air, suspended by invisible force. Her shadow wrapped around her limbs, her throat, her chest. Her eyes rolled back. Her voice broke.

"Roman… help me…"

Roman reached for her.

The Entity's voice echoed through the world.

"She is the Herald.

She is the Key.

She is the Door."

Langley screamed.

Her shadow surged.

Her body twisted.

Her aura darkened.

Roman roared:

"LANGLEY! FIGHT IT!"

She looked at him — just for a moment — and he saw her.

His sister.

Terrified.

Breaking.

"Rome… I'm sorry…"

Her shadow swallowed her whole.

THE ENTITY CLAIMS HER

The Entity stepped forward and placed its hand on Langley's chest.

Her body went still.

Her eyes turned completely black.

Her voice became a whisper of the void.

"I serve."

Roman's heart shattered.

"No… Langley… no…"

The Entity finally turned toward him.

Its voice was a cold, empty truth.

"You rejected the throne.
She did not."

Roman's aura flared violently.

"You can't have her."

The Entity tilted its head.

"She is already mine."

Langley stepped forward — not as Roman's sister.

As the Entity's Herald.

Her shadow stretched toward Roman like a blade.

CHAPTER 26 — ROMAN DEFIES THE ENTITY - *THE FIGHT FOR LANGLEY'S SOUL BEGINS*

Langley stood beside the Entity, her body rigid, her eyes black voids, her shadow stretching across the ruins like a living wound. She wasn't breathing. She wasn't blinking.

She wasn't **herself**.

Roman stepped forward, divine aura blazing around him like a storm of white fire.

"Langley… look at me."

She didn't move.

The Entity tilted its head — a gesture that felt like mockery despite having no face.

"She cannot hear you."

Roman clenched his fists.

"You don't get to take her."

The Entity's voice was a whisper of inevitability.

"She was always mine."

Roman's aura flared violently.

"No.

She's my sister."

The Entity stepped closer, its form flickering like a glitch in reality.

"She is the Herald.

She is the Key.

She is the Door."

Roman's voice cracked.

"She's Langley."

ROMAN STRIKES FIRST

Roman lunged.

A blast of divine energy erupted from his palm, slamming into the Entity with enough force to crack the pavement and shatter nearby windows.

The light swallowed the Entity whole.

James shielded his face.

"Roman—!"

The blast faded.

The Entity stood untouched.

Not burned.

Not damaged.

Not moved.

It didn't even acknowledge the attack.

Roman's breath caught.

"…no way…"

The Entity finally turned its faceless void toward him.

"You cannot strike what does not exist."

Roman's aura surged brighter.

"Then I'll make you exist."

ROMAN TRIES TO BREAK THE BOND

Roman reached for Langley — not physically, but with his power. His aura wrapped around her like a warm, blinding light, pushing against the shadow binding her.

Langley's body convulsed.

Her voice cracked.

"Rome… don't—"

Roman stepped closer.

"I'm right here. I'm not leaving you."

The Entity raised a hand.

Langley screamed.

Her shadow tightened around her like chains, pulling her back toward the Entity.

Roman roared:

"LET HER GO!"

He unleashed a shockwave of divine force that shook the entire block.

The Entity didn't move.

Langley did.

She was thrown backward, slamming into the Entity's grasp like a puppet yanked by invisible strings.

Her voice broke.

"Roman… please… stop…"

Roman froze.

Because she wasn't begging him to stop hurting her.

She was begging him to stop hurting **himself**.

THE ENTITY TIGHTENS ITS HOLD

The Entity placed its hand on Langley's shoulder.

Her body went still.

Her shadow expanded, swallowing the ground beneath her feet.

The Entity spoke:

"She is bound.
She is chosen.
She is mine."

Roman stepped forward, shaking with fury.

"No.
She's Sane.

She's blood.

She's family."

The Entity tilted its head.

"Blood is irrelevant.

Only purpose matters."

Roman's aura exploded outward.

"THEN I'LL CHANGE HER PURPOSE!"

The Entity's voice deepened — not louder, but heavier, like gravity choosing a direction.

"You cannot free what does not wish to be freed."

Roman's heart stopped.

"…Langley…?"

Langley looked at him.

Her eyes were empty.

Her voice was hollow.

"I serve."

Roman staggered backward.

"No… no, Langley… don't say that…"

She stepped toward him.

Her shadow rose like a blade.

"I serve the Void."

ROMAN MAKES HIS CHOICE

Roman wiped blood from his lip.

His aura flared brighter than ever — white fire swirling around him, cracking the ground, bending the air.

He whispered:

"I'm not losing you too."

He raised his hand.

Divine energy surged.

James shouted:

"ROMAN, WAIT—!"

Roman didn't wait.

He charged the Entity.

He charged the darkness.

He charged the impossible.

He charged for Langley.

CHAPTER 27 - LANGLEY ATTACKS ROMAN - *THE ENTITY'S COMMAND*

Langley stood beside the Entity, her body rigid, her eyes black voids, her shadow stretching across the ruins like a living wound. Roman stepped toward her, divine aura blazing.

"Langley… look at me."

She didn't.

The Entity did.

Its faceless void tilted toward Roman.

"Herald."

Langley's body jerked violently.

"Strike."

Her shadow surged.

And she moved.

THE FIRST STRIKE — SHADOW LASH

Langley vanished.

Roman barely had time to react before a tendril of shadow whipped across his chest, sending him crashing through a half-collapsed wall. Dust exploded around him.

James shouted:

"ROMAN!"

Roman rose slowly, divine light flickering around him.

"Langley… don't do this."

She appeared in front of him — inches away — her face twisted with pain and emptiness.

Her voice was layered, broken.

"I don't want to."

Her shadow said:

"I do."

She struck again.

THE SECOND STRIKE — SHADOW SPEAR

A spear of pure darkness formed in Langley's hand. She hurled it at Roman with enough force to crack the pavement beneath her feet.

Roman raised his arm.

A shield of white fire formed around him.

The spear hit.

The explosion shook the entire block.

Roman slid backward, boots carving trenches in the ground.

He gritted his teeth.

"Langley, fight it!"

She screamed — a sound of agony and obedience.

"I CAN'T!"

Her shadow screamed with her.

"YOU WON'T!"

THE THIRD STRIKE — HERALD'S DESCENT

Langley shot into the air, her shadow expanding behind her like wings made of smoke and teeth. She dove toward Roman at impossible speed.

Roman braced.

She hit him like a meteor.

The ground cratered beneath them.

Shockwaves rippled outward.

Cars flipped.

Windows shattered.

Roman coughed blood.

"Langley— please—"

She pinned him to the ground, her hand around his throat, her shadow coiling around his limbs like chains.

Her voice cracked.

"Rome… I'm sorry…"

The Entity's voice echoed through her.

"Break him."

Langley's grip tightened.

Roman's vision blurred.

ROMAN REFUSES TO FIGHT HER

Roman didn't strike back.

He didn't unleash divine fire.
He didn't blast her away.
He didn't defend himself.

He placed his hand on her cheek.

"Langley… I'm not fighting you."

Her eyes flickered — black, then silver, then black again.

Her voice trembled.

"Don't… make me hurt you…"

Roman whispered:

"You're not hurting me.
He is."

Langley's body convulsed.

Her shadow screamed.

The Entity stepped closer.

**"Herald.
Finish him."**

Langley's hand tightened around Roman's throat.

Her shadow raised a blade.

Roman whispered:

"I love you, Lang."

Langley froze.

Just for a heartbeat.

Just long enough for the Entity to react.

THE ENTITY FORCES HER HAND

The Entity's voice boomed through the ruins.

"OBEY."

Langley screamed — a sound of pure torment — and her shadow blade plunged downward toward Roman's chest.

Roman closed his eyes.

He didn't move.

He didn't defend.

He didn't strike back.

Because he wasn't fighting Langley.

He was fighting the thing inside her.

CHAPTER 28 - JAMES INTERVENES - *THE MOMENT BEFORE THE KILLING BLOW*

Langley's shadow blade plunged downward toward Roman's chest.

Roman didn't move.

He didn't defend.

He whispered:

"Langley… I'm not fighting you."

Her eyes flickered — black, then silver, then black again.

Her voice cracked.

"I can't stop—"

The Entity's voice boomed through her:

"FINISH HIM."

The blade descended.

And James moved.

JAMES THROWS HIMSELF BETWEEN THEM

James didn't think.

Didn't plan.

Didn't hesitate.

He sprinted across the rubble, lungs burning, ribs screaming, boots slipping on ash and broken stone.

He dove.

And slammed into Roman, knocking him out of the blade's path.

The shadow blade hit the ground where Roman's heart had been — carving a crater into the pavement.

Roman gasped.

"JAMES—!"

James rolled, coughing blood, vision swimming.

"Get… up… Rome…"

Langley froze.

Her shadow twitched violently.

Her voice trembled.

"James… move…"

James staggered to his feet, standing between her and Roman.

He raised his weapon — empty, useless, shaking.

"I'm not letting you kill him."

THE ENTITY REACTS

The Entity tilted its faceless void toward James.

The air grew colder.
The shadows deepened.
The world dimmed.

"Irrelevant."

James felt something press against his mind — a crushing, suffocating pressure that made his knees buckle.

Roman grabbed his shoulder.

"James, get back—"

James shoved him away.

"No.
I'm done running."

Langley's body jerked violently, like a puppet pulled by too many strings.

Her voice broke.

"James... please... don't..."

The Entity whispered:

"Herald.

Remove him."

Langley screamed.

Her shadow surged.

LANGLEY STRIKES AT JAMES

She vanished.

Reappeared behind him.

Her hand wrapped around his throat.

Her shadow coiled around his chest like a serpent.

James choked, feet lifting off the ground.

Roman roared:

"LANGLEY, STOP!"

Langley's eyes flickered — black, then silver, then black again.

Her voice cracked.

"I don't want to hurt you…"

James gasped.

"Then… don't…"

Her grip tightened.

The Entity's voice echoed:

"Obey."

Langley's shadow constricted.

James's vision blurred.

Roman's divine aura flared violently.

"LANGLEY, LET HIM GO!"

ROMAN SAVES JAMES — AND REACHES LANGLEY

Roman unleashed a blast of divine force — not at Langley, but at the **shadow** holding James.

The shadow shattered.

James fell, gasping, collapsing into Roman's arms.

Langley staggered backward, clutching her head, screaming.

Her voice split into two:

"STOP—"
"OBEY—"

Roman stood, placing James gently on the ground.

He stepped toward Langley.

His aura blazed white.

"Langley… look at me."

She did.

And for the first time since the Entity claimed her…

He saw her.

Her real eyes.

Her real fear.

Her real pain.

"Rome… help me…"

Roman reached out his hand.

"I'm right here."

The Entity's voice thundered:

"ENOUGH."

Langley's body snapped upright.

Her eyes went black again.

Her shadow surged.

And she lunged at Roman.

CHAPTER 29 — THE BREAKING POINT - *JAMES DEATH AND ROMAN'S ASCENSCION*

The moment Langley lunged at Roman, her shadow blade raised, the Entity's command echoing through her—

"FINISH HIM."

—James moved again.

He didn't shout.
He didn't hesitate.
He didn't think.

He just *acted.*

He threw himself between them.

Roman's eyes widened.

"JAMES—!"

Langley's blade struck.

There was no blood spray.
No gore.
Just a sudden, terrible stillness.

James gasped, eyes wide, breath catching in his throat.

He looked at Roman.

"…I told you… I got you…"

And he collapsed.

Roman caught him before he hit the ground.

"James— James, stay with me—"

James's hand trembled against Roman's chest.

"Don't… let her… be alone…"

His eyes dimmed.

His hand fell.

And James — Roman's brother in everything but blood — was gone.

ROMAN BREAKS

Roman didn't scream.

He didn't cry.

He didn't collapse.

He *changed.*

The divine light inside him didn't flare — it detonated.

The ground cracked beneath him.

The air rippled outward.

The sky split open.

Langley staggered backward, her shadow recoiling like it had been burned.

The Entity tilted its head.

Roman rose slowly, James's body in his arms, his aura burning white-hot.

His voice was quiet.

Too quiet.

"You killed him."

The Entity answered:

"Irrelevant."

Roman's aura exploded.

ROMAN GOES ALL OUT

He set James gently on the ground.

Then he turned toward Langley and the Entity.

His eyes glowed like twin suns.

His veins pulsed with light.

His shadow was gone — replaced by a halo of raw creation.

He whispered:

“I warned you.”

The world reacted.

The pavement cracked.

The sky thundered.

The air vibrated with divine force.

Roman moved.

He didn’t run.

He didn’t leap.

He simply *appeared* in front of Langley.

She swung her shadow blade.

Roman caught it with his bare hand.

The blade shattered.

Langley gasped — her real voice breaking through.

“Rome— I can’t—”

Roman touched her forehead.

A blast of light erupted.

Langley screamed — not in pain, but in *separation* — the Entity's influence ripping away from her piece by piece.

The Entity stepped forward.

"ENOUGH."

Roman turned toward it.

And struck.

THE ENTITY IS WOUNDED

Roman's fist — glowing with divine fire — connected with the Entity's chest.

For the first time since its awakening…

The Entity *reacted.*

Its form flickered violently.

Its void-face cracked like glass.

Its voice distorted.

"Impossible—"

Roman didn't stop.

He struck again.

And again.

And again.

Each blow shook the city.

Each blow tore reality.

Each blow weakened the Entity.

Langley collapsed to her knees, clutching her head, the darkness peeling off her like smoke.

"Rome… stop… you'll tear the world apart—"

Roman didn't hear her.

He was beyond hearing.

Beyond restraint.

Beyond mercy.

LANGLEY IS MORTALLY WOUNDED

The Entity, desperate, lashed out — not at Roman, but at Langley.

A tendril of void energy struck her in the chest.

She gasped, collapsed, her shadow flickering violently.

Roman froze.

"LANGLEY!"

He caught her before she hit the ground.

Her eyes — no longer black, no longer void — looked up at him.

"Rome… I'm sorry…"

Roman's voice cracked.

"No. No, stay with me—"

The Entity staggered, its form collapsing inward.

"She… is… mine…"

Roman's aura flared so brightly the world turned white.

"No."

He stood.

Langley in his arms.

James at his feet.

The Entity dying before him.

Roman whispered:

"She was never yours."

And he unleashed everything.

AFTERMATH — ALL THREE FALL

When the light faded:

- The Entity lay shattered, its form broken, its void-face cracked open.

- Langley lay unconscious in Roman's arms, her breathing shallow, her life fading.
- Roman stood barely upright, his divine aura flickering, his body trembling from the power he unleashed.

He looked at James's body.

Then at Langley.

Then at the dying Entity.

And Roman — divine, furious, grieving — whispered:

"This ends with me."

CHAPTER 30 — THE FALL OF THE SANES - *CORINNE ARRIVES AT THE END OF THE WORLD*

The battlefield was still trembling from Roman's last attack when a voice cut through the smoke — raw, desperate, terrified.

"ROMAN!"

He turned.

Corinne — armor scorched, uniform torn, eyes burning with determination — sprinted toward him with a squad of surviving soldiers behind her. They looked like they'd crawled out of the apocalypse itself.

But Corinne didn't see the ruins.

She saw **Roman**.

She saw **Langley**.

She saw the **Entity**.

And Roman saw something too.

He froze.

His divine aura flickered violently.

"…Corinne…?"

The Entity turned its faceless void toward her.

And both Roman and the Entity sensed it at the same time.

Four heartbeats.

Four life forces.

Four Sane children.

Corinne didn't know.

Roman didn't know.

But the Entity did.

And it reacted with pure, ancient terror.

THE ENTITY TRIES TO ERASE THE FUTURE

The Entity's voice cracked the air like a cosmic blade.

"THE CHILDREN MUST NOT LIVE."

A spear of void energy formed in its hand — aimed directly at Corinne's stomach.

Roman moved instantly.

He threw himself in front of her, divine aura flaring into a shield of white fire.

The void spear hit.

The shield shattered like glass under a hammer.

Roman staggered, coughing, but stayed standing.

Corinne grabbed his arm.

"Roman— what's happening—?"

He looked at her stomach.

Then at her eyes.

And whispered:

"...our children..."

Corinne froze.

"What...?"

The Entity roared.

"HERALD.
STRIKE."

Langley jerked violently, her body snapping upright like a puppet pulled by invisible strings.

Her eyes went black.

Her shadow formed a blade.

Roman turned—

"LANGLEY, NO—"

LANGLEY STRIKES ROMAN

Langley plunged the dark blade into Roman's chest.

There was no gore — but the *impact* was catastrophic.

Roman's body jerked.

His aura shattered like a dying star.

The ground cracked beneath him.

Corinne screamed — a raw, animal sound.

"ROMAN!"

Langley's eyes flickered — black, then silver, then black again.

Her voice cracked, horrified.

"No… no, no, no— what did I—"

Roman collapsed into her arms.

She caught him, trembling, shaking, breaking.

"Rome… I didn't… I didn't mean—"

Roman touched her cheek weakly.

"Lang… it wasn't you…"

She shook her head violently, tears streaming.

"I hurt you… I hurt James… I hurt everyone…"

Roman's voice was fading.

"Langley… listen… Corinne… she's pregnant…"

Langley looked at Corinne's stomach.

Her breath caught.

Her face broke.

"Oh God… I'm so sorry…"

The Entity's voice thundered:

"HERALD.

RETURN."

Langley screamed as the darkness clawed at her mind again.

She looked at Roman.

Then at Corinne.

Then at the Entity.

And she made her choice.

LANGLEY'S SACRIFICE

Langley stood.

Her shadow writhed violently, trying to pull her back under the Entity's control.

She fought it.

She fought *him*.

She fought **herself**.

She whispered to Corinne:

"Protect them."

Then she turned the shadow blade on herself.

Corinne screamed.

"LANGLEY— NO—!"

Langley smiled through tears.

"Tell them… I loved them… even before they existed…"

And she ended her own life.

Her body fell beside Roman's.

The Entity shrieked — a sound of pure, cosmic fury — as its Herald severed the bond by force.

Its form cracked.

Its power collapsed.

Its existence unraveled.

Roman reached for Langley's hand.

She reached for his.

They died together.

Brother and sister.

Light and shadow.

Sane and Herald.

THE SANES' ESSENCE PASSES ON

Corinne dropped to her knees beside Roman, sobbing uncontrollably.

"Roman— please— please don't leave me—"

Roman lifted a trembling hand and touched her cheek.

Then her stomach.

"I love you…
and our children…"

His hand fell.

His eyes dimmed.

Roman Sane died.

A surge of divine and shadow essence erupted from Roman and Langley's bodies — swirling together, merging, becoming something new.

The energy flowed into Corinne's stomach.

Her unborn children glowed with light.

A shockwave blasted outward across the world:

- The skies tore open and cleared.
- The Between sealed shut.
- The undead collapsed mid-charge.
- The corruption evaporated like smoke.

The Entity's remains dissolved into nothing.

The world breathed again.

THE GODLIKE VISITOR

A figure of pure light descended before Corinne — tall, radiant, impossible to look at directly.

Its voice was calm.

"The war is not over.

But today…

you have won the battle."

Corinne clutched her stomach, tears streaming.

"Roman… Langley…"

The divine being bowed its head.

"Their legacy lives within you."

And it vanished.

EPILOGUE — THE WORLD BEGINS TO HEAL

Scenes flashed across the world:

- Soldiers pushing back the undead with renewed strength.
- Survivors reclaiming streets once lost.
- The infected collapsing as the corruption died.
- Humanity is rising again.

And then—

Corinne.

Walking out of the battlefield.

Smoke behind her.
Gunfire in the distance.
Her hand on her stomach.
Her face streaked with tears and ash.

But her eyes?

Determined.

Unbroken.

Carrying the future of the Sane bloodline.

The scene ends.

BOOK II — CHAPTER 1 — THE WORLD REBUILDS - *THE FIRST DAWN AFTER THE END*

The shockwave from Roman and Langley's sacrifice had rolled across the planet like a cleansing tide.
When it faded, the world was left in a silence it hadn't heard in years.

Not the silence of death.

The silence of **possibility**.

GLOBAL AFTERMATH — HUMANITY RISES

Across the world, people emerged from bunkers, barricades, collapsed buildings, and ruined cities. They stepped into sunlight that hadn't touched the earth in months.

The skies were clear.
The air was warm.
The Between was sealed.

And the undead?

They were collapsing where they stood — bodies falling limp, eyes dimming, the corruption evaporating like smoke.

For the first time in years…

Humanity wasn't losing.

They were **winning**.

AROUND THE WORLD — SCENES OF RECLAMATION

1. New York City

Soldiers pushed through Times Square, clearing the last pockets of undead.
Civilians emerged from subway tunnels, blinking at the sunlight. A little girl pointed at the sky and whispered:

"Mom… the clouds are gone."

2. London

Firefighters and medics worked side by side, pulling survivors from rubble.
Church bells rang — not for mourning, but for hope.

3. Tokyo

Self-Defense Forces marched through Shibuya Crossing, reclaiming the streets.
Digital billboards flickered back to life, broadcasting emergency messages:

"WE SURVIVED."

4. Lagos

Communities formed human chains, clearing debris, rebuilding homes, sharing food.
People sang — tired, broken, but alive.

5. São Paulo

A group of teenagers raised a Brazilian flag over a collapsed highway. One of them whispered:

"For the ones who didn't make it."

THE SANES' LEGACY — A NEW FORCE IN THE WORLD

Everywhere, people felt it:

Warmth in the air.

A pressure in their chests.

A sense of protection.

Roman's divine essence.

Langley's shadow essence.

Both now live inside Corinne's unborn children.

The world didn't know it yet…

But the next generation of Sanes had already begun shaping reality.

THE SURVIVORS — HOPE RETURNS

Hospitals reopened.

Generators roared back to life.

Doctors and nurses worked around the clock.

People who had been bitten but not fully turned... stopped turning.

The corruption inside them dissolved.

Families reunited.
Communities rebuilt.
Humanity remembered what it felt like to hope.

THE LAST BATTLES — HUMANS TAKE BACK THEIR WORLD

Not all undead collapsed.
Some pockets remained — mutated, stubborn, refusing to die.

But now?

Humans weren't afraid.

They fought with renewed strength.
They fought with purpose.
They fought knowing the tide had turned.

And everywhere, soldiers whispered the same thing:

"Roman Sane did this."

CORINNE — THE MOTHER OF THE NEW AGE

Amid the chaos and rebuilding, Corinne walked through the battlefield.

Smoke behind her.

Gunfire in the distance.

Her hand on her stomach.

Her face streaked with tears and ash.

But her eyes?

Determined.

Focused.

Unbreakable.

She wasn't just surviving.

She was carrying the future.

The future Roman and Langley died for.

The future the Entity feared.

The future the world needed.

THE NEW ERA BEGINS

As Corinne stepped into the sunlight, the wind shifted — warm, gentle, almost familiar.

A whisper seemed to echo through the air:

"We're with you."

Roman's voice.

Langley's voice.

The Sane bloodline.

Alive inside her children.

The world was being rebuilt.

And the next chapter?

Was already waiting to be written.

BOOK II — CHAPTER 2 — THE CHILDREN OF THE SANES - *THE FIRST SIGNS OF POWER*

Corinne sat alone in what used to be a field hospital — now a makeshift sanctuary. The world outside was rebuilding, but inside her?

A storm.

Her hand rested on her stomach, feeling the faintest flutter — not movement, but **energy**.

Warm.

Cold.

Light.

Shadow.

All at once.

She whispered:

"...Roman... Langley... what did you leave me with..."

The lights flickered.

Not from power loss.

From **them**.

THE FIRST POWER — THE HEARTBEAT THAT SHAKES REALITY

Corinne felt it first as a pulse.

Then the room felt it.

Then the building.

A single heartbeat — not hers — rippled outward like a shockwave.

The air trembled.

The walls vibrated.

The ground hummed.

The doctor outside stumbled.

"What the hell was that—?"

Corinne clutched her stomach.

The heartbeat pulsed again.

This time, the lights exploded in a burst of white and black sparks — divine and shadow energy mixing in the air.

Corinne gasped.

"…my babies…"

THE SECOND POWER — THE SHADOW THAT PROTECTS

A scream echoed outside.

A stray undead — one of the last — had slipped through the perimeter.

It lunged at a soldier.

Corinne didn't think.

She didn't move.

Her children did.

A shadow erupted from her stomach — not violent, not monstrous — but **precise**.
It shot across the room like a spear of darkness, wrapping around the undead's throat.

The creature froze mid-lunge.

Its body convulsed.

Then it collapsed, lifeless.

The shadow slithered back toward Corinne…

…and disappeared into her.

She whispered:

"…Langley…"

THE THIRD POWER — THE LIGHT THAT HEALS

A medic rushed in, panicked.

"Corinne! Are you okay? The whole building just—"

He stopped.

Corinne's stomach glowed.

Not bright.

Not blinding.

Soft.

Warm.

Alive.

The medic stared.

"Is that… normal?"

Corinne didn't answer.

Because she felt something else.

Her exhaustion faded.

Her wounds closed.

Her breathing steadied.

Her children were healing her.

Roman's gift.

THE FOURTH POWER — THE ECHO OF THE BETWEEN

That night, Corinne dreamed.

But it wasn't a dream.

She stood in a place of white sky and black ground — the Between.

But it wasn't hostile.

It wasn't cold.

It was… waiting.

Four silhouettes stood before her — small, childlike, glowing with swirling light and shadow.

One stepped forward.

A voice echoed in her mind:

"Mother."

Corinne fell to her knees, sobbing.

"Roman… Langley… are you—?"

The child shook its head.

"We are not them.
We are what comes next."

The Between trembled.

The child reached out and touched her hand.

"The world will need us."

Corinne woke up gasping.

Her stomach glowed softly.

The air around her shimmered.

And she whispered:

"...my children... what are you becoming..."

THE WORLD FEELS THEM

Across the planet, people paused.

A sudden warmth in the air.

A pressure in their chest.

A whisper in the wind.

Something new had entered the world.

Something powerful.

Something ancient.

Something Sane.

A soldier in New York whispered:

"Did you feel that...?"

A child in Tokyo looked up at the sky.

"Mom... the light changed."

A priest in Rome dropped his candle.

"The prophecy... it's begun..."

CORINNE UNDERSTANDS THE TRUTH

She stood outside the hospital, hand on her stomach, staring at the sunrise.

Her voice was steady.

Determined.

Unbreakable.

"I'll protect you.
All four of you.
No matter what comes next."

The wind shifted.

Warm.
Cold.
Light.
Shadow.

A whisper echoed around her:

"We know."

BOOK II — CHAPTER 3 — THE NEXT THREAT AWAKENS - *SOMETHING OLD SENSE THE CHILDREN*

The world was rebuilding.

The skies were clear.

The undead were dying out.

But far beyond the Between — deeper than the Entity ever reached — something stirred.

Something that had been waiting.

Watching.

Hungry.

IN THE VOID BEYOND THE BETWEEN

There was no sky here.

No ground.

No time.

Only a vast, endless dark ocean of consciousness — ancient, cold, and patient.

The Entity had been a fragment.

A scout.

A whisper.

But the thing that now opened its eyes?

It was the **source**.

A presence older than the first Ending.

Older than the throne.

Older than the Sane bloodline itself.

It felt the shockwave of Roman and Langley's death.

It felt the sealing of the Between.

It felt the world healing.

And then—

It felt **them**.

Four heartbeats.

Four lights.

Four shadows.

Four impossibilities.

The children.

The next generation of Sane.

The presence rippled through the void.

"They live."

THE CHILDREN'S POWER REACHES THE VOID

Corinne slept in a reclaimed military shelter, with one hand on her stomach.

Her children dreamed.

And their dreams were not human.

One child dreamed of light — a blinding, divine radiance that pierced the void like a spear.

Another dreamed of shadowing a swirling vortex that bent reality around it.

A third dreamed of the Between — reshaping it like clay.

The fourth dreamed of something new — something neither Roman nor Langley ever possessed.

A power the void had never seen.

Their dreams echoed outward.

Across the world.

Across the Between.

Across the void.

The ancient presence felt every heartbeat.

Every pulse.

Every spark.

And it whispered:

"The bloodline evolves."

THE PRESENCE REACTS

The void trembled.

Not with fear.

With anticipation.

"The Herald is dead.

The Divine is dead.

But their legacy…

their spawn…"

The presence expanded, stretching across the void like a storm of consciousness.

"…they will not be allowed to rise."

It reached the Between.

But the Between was sealed.

The presence recoiled, hissing.

"The door is closed."

It paused.

Then smiled — though it had no face.

"Doors can be broken."

ON EARTH — PEOPLE FEEL IT

Across the world, survivors paused.

A sudden chill.

A pressure in the air.

A whisper in the wind.

A soldier in New York shivered.

"Did you feel that…?"

A child in Tokyo clutched her chest.

"Mom… something's watching us."

A priest in Rome dropped to his knees.

"The darkness… it's shifting…"

The world didn't know what it was.

But they felt it.

Something had noticed the children.

Something powerful.

Something ancient.

Something worse than the Entity.

CORINNE FEELS IT TOO

Corinne woke with a gasp.

Her stomach pulsed — not painfully, but urgently.

Her children were awake.

And afraid.

She whispered:

"…what's wrong…?"

A voice echoed in her mind — not hers, not Roman's, not Langley's.

One of the children.

"Mother… something is coming."

Corinne froze.

"What is it?"

The child answered with a whisper that chilled her blood.

"The one the Entity served."

Corinne's breath caught.

Her hand tightened on her stomach.

"…Roman… Langley… what did you leave me to face…"

The wind outside shifted.

Cold.

Heavy.

Watching.

The presence whispered through the world:

"I am coming for them."

BOOK II — CHAPTER 4 — THE DOOR THAT SHOULD NOT OPEN - *THE ANCIENT PRESENCE TRIES TO BREAK THROUGH*

The void beyond the Between churned like a storm made of thought and hunger.
The ancient presence — older than the Entity, older than the throne, older than the first Ending — stretched itself across the darkness.

It had no form.
No face.
No mercy.

But it had **purpose**.

And it whispered:

"The children live."

The void trembled.

"The bloodline evolves."

A pulse of power rippled outward — a shockwave that cracked the edges of reality like ice under pressure.

The presence pressed its will against the sealed Between.

The barrier glowed white.

Then black.

Then white again.

The presence hissed.

"A door is a suggestion."

It struck.

Reality buckled.

The Between screamed.

The seal flickered.

On Earth, Corinne gasped — her children twisting inside her, sensing the attack.

One whispered in her mind:

"Mother… it's trying to come through…"

Corinne clutched her stomach.

"Not while I'm alive."

The presence struck again.

Harder.

The Between cracked like glass.

A sliver of void leaked through — cold, ancient, hungry.

The presence whispered:

"I am coming."

The crack widened.

The world trembled.

And then—

Everything went silent.

CUT TO — THE GODLIKE KINGDOM - *ROMAN AND LANGLEY WAKE UP SOMEWHERE IMPOSSIBLE*

Light.

Warm.

Soft.

Endless.

Roman opened his eyes.

He was lying on a field of shimmering gold grass, each blade glowing like a tiny star. A warm breeze brushed his face. The sky above him was a swirling tapestry of white, gold, and soft violet — alive, breathing, divine.

He sat up slowly.

His chest didn't hurt.

His body wasn't broken.

He was whole.

"Where… am I…"

A voice answered behind him.

"Rome..."

He turned.

Langley stood there — alive, unscarred, radiant. Her hair flowed like liquid shadow and light at the same time. Her eyes were no longer void or corrupt.

They were hers.

Roman stood, stunned.

"Lang... you're—"

She nodded, tears in her eyes.

"I think we made it somewhere... else."

They looked around.

The kingdom stretched endlessly — mountains made of crystal, rivers of light, trees that shimmered with divine energy. The air hummed with power.

Roman whispered:

"...is this heaven?"

Langley shook her head slowly.

"No.
This is older."

A figure appeared on a distant hill — tall, radiant, impossible to look at directly.

The same divine being who spoke to Corinne.

It raised a hand.

And spoke without sound:

"Welcome, children of the Sane.
Your story is not over."

Roman and Langley exchanged a look — fear, awe, confusion, hope.

The being stepped closer.

"The world below faces a new enemy.
And you…
are not done fighting."

The sky rumbled.

The golden grass rippled.

The divine kingdom pulsed with power.

Roman whispered:

"…Corinne…"

Langley whispered:

"…the children…"

The being smiled — or something like it.

"To be continued."